Return to
Val Clentone
125 Olney Que.
N. Prov. RI
Cell: (401) 484-2125

THE DEAD MAN IN THE BUNKER

MARTIN POLLACK

The Dead Man in the Bunker

Discovering my father

TRANSLATED BY WILL HOBSON

faber and faber

First published as *Der Tote im Bunker* in 2004
by Paul Zsolnay Verlag Wien
First published in Great Britain in 2006
by Faber and Faber Limited
3 Queen Square London WC1N 3AU

Typeset by Faber and Faber Ltd
Printed in England by Mackays of Chatham, plc

A CIP record for this book
is available from the British Library

ISBN 0–571–22800–3
ISBN 978–0–571–22800–3

2 4 6 8 10 9 7 5 3 1

MAPS

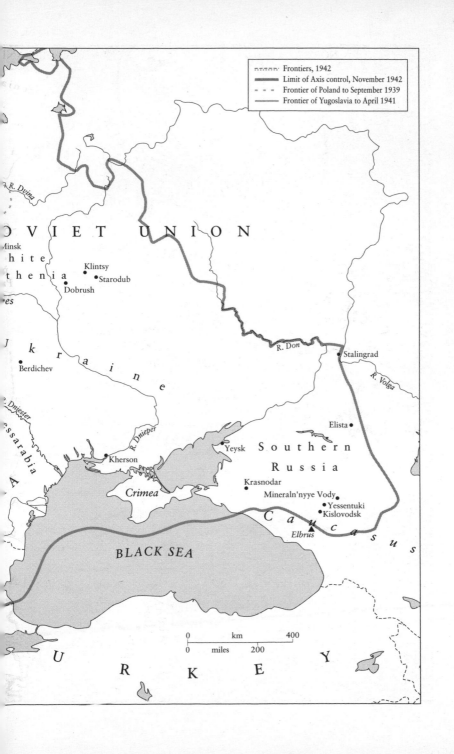

Frontiers, 1942
Limit of Axis control, November 1942
Frontier of Poland to September 1939
Frontier of Yugoslavia to April 1941

SOVIET UNION

Minsk

White
Ruthenia
es

Klintsy
Starodub
Dobrush

R. Dvina

Ukraine

Berdichev

R. Dniester

Bessarabia

A

Kherson

R. Dnieper

Crimea

Yeysk

R. Don

Stalingrad

R. Volga

Elista

Southern
Russia

Krasnodar

Mineraln'nyye Vody
Yessentuki
Kislovodsk

Caucasus

Elbrus

BLACK SEA

0   km   400
0   miles   200

TURKEY

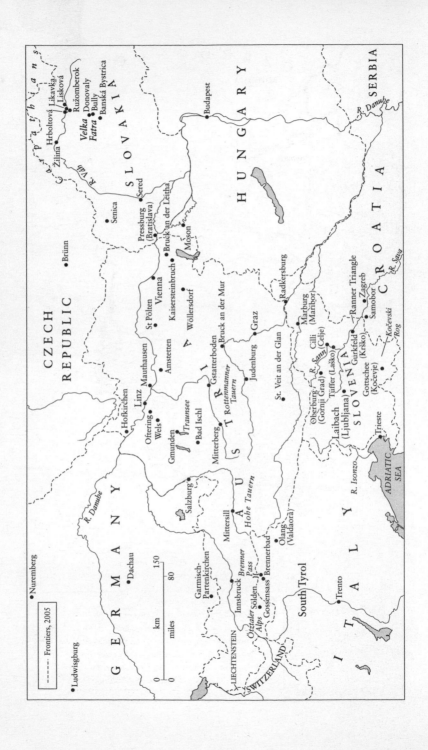

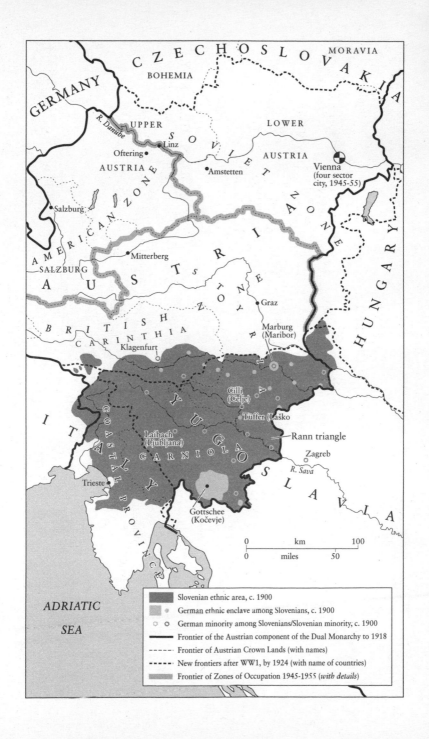

GERMANY

CZECHOSLOVAKIA

BOHEMIA

MORAVIA

UPPER

LOWER

R. Danube

Oftering •

• Linz

AUSTRIA

SOVIET ZONE

Amstetten •

Vienna
(four sector
city, 1945-55)

AMERICAN ZONE

• Salzburg

SALZBURG

A U S T R I A

Mitterberg •

Styria

ZONE

• Graz

BRITISH

CARINTHIA

Marburg
(Maribor)

Klagenfurt ○

Y U G O S L A V I A

Cilli
(Celje)

Tuffer (Laško)

Laibach
(Ljubljana)

CARNIOLA

Rann triangle

Zagreb

R. Sava

Trieste •

COASTAL PROVINCE

Gottschee
(Kočevje)

ITALY

| 0 | | km | | 100 |
| 0 | miles | | 50 | |

ADRIATIC

SEA

Slovenian ethnic area, c. 1900

German ethnic enclave among Slovenians, c. 1900

German minority among Slovenians/Slovenian minority, c. 1900

Frontier of the Austrian component of the Dual Monarchy to 1918

Frontier of Austrian Crown Lands (with names)

New frontiers after WW1, by 1924 (with name of countries)

Frontier of Zones of Occupation 1945-1955 (*with details*)

In the early summer of 2003, I drove with my wife to the South Tyrol, to the Brenner Pass, to look for the bunker in which my father had been found dead fifty-six years before. I knew he had been shot, but I wanted to find out more about how he had died and what had brought him to the South Tyrol. I had put off the investigation for years, perhaps from an unconscious feeling of dread that in trying to trace him I might come across things that would exceed my, in any case bad, expectations. One thing I knew from the outset: his violent death was the conclusion of a life governed by violence.

We had arranged to meet a man in a café on Gossensass's market square who had promised to help us look for the bunker. Peter Kaser is an artist who devotes his spare time to exploring the Italian fortifications along the Brenner border. He has turned one of these disused bunkers into an art space for performances and installations, which he manages himself. We learnt that there are over fifty bunkers and casemates on the Italian side of the Brenner, which Mussolini had built between 1936 and 1942 as the *Sbarramento am Brenner*, the Barrier on the Brenner, to defend against Austria and Germany, although naturally the fortifications never played any military role. Everyone we asked knew the story of the body in the bunker – it had been much discussed at the time – but no one could say where it had happened. They said that there were a lot of bunkers in the area, and that all that was a long time ago. Finally we came across an old man, with the round, rosy face of a child, who might help. He said that he lived not far from the bunker in question and that his father often used to tell him about the discovery of the body. The incident had shaken up the whole valley back then, even though people were pretty well numbed so soon after the war. At first he didn't want to reveal the whereabouts of the bunker. He explained that his father had forbidden him to talk about those events; that he'd just get his fingers burnt if he did, and saying this, he broke into a mischievous smile, like a child who gets his fun from stalling people and keeping them in suspense. But Kaser persisted until finally the old man divulged the information.

We reached the place he'd directed us to along a narrow road running parallel to the motorway, within sight of the railway station on the Brenner Pass. From the motorway came a roar that swelled and subsided, amplified by the sides of the valley, which acted like a funnel. Beside the road there was a flat strip of marshy pasture and beyond that woods that climbed steeply uphill, spruce and larch interspersed with the occasional alder and birch. After a few steps, we stumbled across some rusty barbed wire, hidden by thick acanthus leaves and thistles so that it looked like part of the lush vegetation. 'This is right,' Kaser said. 'Wherever you find barbed wire, there'll be a bunker somewhere nearby.' We steered around clumps of tall stinging nettles, dark islands in the bright green foliage, stirring up clouds of tiny midges from the undergrowth at every step. On the opposite slope of the mountain, a lean man was mowing a steep field with broad swinging strokes, his tanned upper body glistening with sweat. He had taken off his white shirt and put it down at the edge of the meadow; from a distance it looked like a dog. Under the spruces at the edge of the wood there was a black metal sign with the faded bilingual inscription *'Proprietà Militare: Accesso vietato. Militäreigentum: Zutritt verboten'* ('Military Property: No Admittance'). We came to a low, overgrown stone wall, behind which there was a rock shelter with a cleft running from top to bottom. It was a gate, standing open a crack, artfully made out of grey-green fibreglass mats, with bulges and folds, so that to a cursory glance it might look like living rock. The gate opened surprisingly easily. The whole thing had something of the entrance to an old-fashioned ghost train about it, except that here we were in the middle of the countryside, at the foot of a steep, thickly wooded slope. The gate gave onto a small space, two metres by two metres, with mossy, damp concrete walls and a ceiling also made of fibreglass. In the front wall, there was an iron door painted green and reinforced with thick bars, with a peephole covered by a cast-iron flap at eye level. The door was welded shut. We were standing in front of the bunker in which my father's body had been found on 6 April 1947.

We set off into the wood to see if we could find another way in. Peter Kaser explained that, for safety reasons, military bunkers generally had two entrances. The slope, thickly covered with needles, was slippery, and we had to hold onto the low-hanging branches in order not to lose our footing. A dark mound ten metres above the entrance proved to be part of the underground complex. A concrete ring projecting about twelve inches above

ground supported a rusty cupola with barred observation slits that gave off a strong smell of mould. A lookout. It must have been possible once to survey the whole valley as far as the Austrian border from there, but now tall spruces blocked the view. We discovered a second lookout some distance away, and later we found a plan of the bunker in a book about the fortifications on the Brenner: Opera 2, Works No. 2, a medium-sized bunker equipped with two machine guns and an anti-tank gun. But we didn't find a second entrance, only an old, neglected path overgrown with bushes and trees. It was maybe thirty or forty metres from the path to the entrance of the bunker, steeply downhill all the way through the wood. It can't have been difficult dragging a lifeless body down there unseen. Presumably my father was shot up on the path.

The body was discovered on a Sunday by the wife of an Italian railway worker stationed on the Brenner, who was taking a walk with her husband and son in the direction of the Albergo al Lupo, the Brenner Wolf Inn. The boy had spotted something unusual among the trees; perhaps the imitation rock gate was open then too. He had worked his way down through the deep snow, and his mother had followed. It is not clear why she went into the bunker, which was still open at the time – whether out of curiosity or whether because, despite the winter cold, a smell of decay hung in the air – but she came upon the body just inside the entrance. Called to the scene, the *carabinieri* immediately established that it was murder: the dead man had two bullet wounds in the head and one in the chest. He had clearly been lying in the bunker for a considerable time. A few meagre belongings and papers scattered in front of the entrance were presumed to be his, among them an ethnic German identity card issued in the name of Franz Geyer, a worker from the Slovenian town of Krško, which was called Gurkfeld in German. He had no money or valuables on him. Even at that first examination, however, doubts arose about his identity. He had a small tattoo on the inside of his left upper arm and scars on his face, like those worn by *Burschenschafter*, members of student duelling fraternities. This hardly fitted a worker. Enquiries to the Austrian police authorities in Innsbruck revealed that the identity card was forged. The dead man wasn't an ethnic German from Gurkfeld but the Austrian Dr Gerhard Bast, SS Sturmbannführer (Major), born on 12 January 1911 in what was then called Gottschee, in Yugoslavia, with right of domicile in Amstetten in Lower Austria. He was wanted by Linz Federal Police Head Office as a war criminal, having been chief of the Linz Gestapo for a considerable time. He was my father.

Weeks after the discovery of the body, a detective came to see my grandmother in Oftering, a small place near Linz in the American zone of occupation, where she and her husband had fled to from Amstetten to escape the Russians. The officer asked if my grandmother had a picture of her son Gerhard; it was needed to establish the identity of a murder victim. This was how she discovered that her son had been robbed and murdered on the Brenner. My grandmother didn't have a picture of her son, so the policeman asked her to travel with an officer to South Tyrol to identify the dead man. When they arrived, he was already buried. The *carabinieri* requested that grandmother perform the identification from photographs they had taken of the murdered man. She refused, saying she didn't want to look at those pictures under any circumstances. Then the *carabinieri* asked if her son had two scars on his face, on the left cheek. This she confirmed: they were indeed scars from student duels. My grandmother also recognized some of the objects presented to her as her son's property, among them a fountain pen, a watch and a slim notebook covered in blue plastic that he had used as a journal. It bore his name in Gothic script on the first page and the words 'Begun on 1 January 1937.' These details and pieces of circumstantial evidence were enough for the Italian authorities to issue a death certificate. Later his file said that the dead man was identified by his mother, but she always insisted on spelling out that she had neither been an eyewitness to her son's death nor seen him dead. It almost sounded as if, against her better judgement, she was clinging to the hope that the events on the Brenner might still be resolved as a tragic case of mistaken identity.

When I drove to the South Tyrol with my wife, I had with me a photo of the grave in which the dead man had been buried in April 1947 in the municipality of Brennero: a narrow mound edged with rough stones and a white headstone that, besides giving the dead man's name and dates of birth and death, said that he had been a Protestant. After our trip to the bunker we visited the pretty little graveyard that hugs St Valentine's, the Catholic church, with its Romanesque tower pointing sternly skywards. The graveyard contains a few dozen graves, all there is room for

within the high walls that shield it from the clamour of the busy border town. The names on the headstones and wrought iron crosses are mostly German, a few Italian; my father's grave no longer exists. His remains were exhumed in the 1960s at my grandmother's request and transferred to Amstetten. I remember the funeral in the small Lower Austrian town; I had been allowed out especially from my boarding school near Salzburg. My overriding memory is of how uncomfortable I felt and how I had to struggle not to appear unmoved to my Amstetten relatives and the dead man's friends, who observed me sympathetically as I stood before the open grave.

I have no real memories of my father. I wasn't yet three when he died and I had only seen him fleetingly a few times. Even that I only know from my mother, who rarely spoke about him, and then only about harmless things, trivialities, as if she weren't sure what she could confide in me and what it would be better to keep to herself.

2

My father was born in 1911 in Gottschee, in what was then the crownland of Carniola in the Habsburg Empire. He could not be called a genuine Gottscheer, however, because his parents were immigrants who only lived for a few years in the centre of this German-speaking enclave in what is now Slovenia. My grandfather had moved there in 1907 from another small town called Tüffer, in the neighbouring crownland of Styria, to work as a trainee in an established law firm. I don't know how he came to choose Gottschee, or Kočevje, as it is known in Slovenian. He had studied law in Graz. A year later my grandmother was transferred to Gottschee to take up her first teaching position in the girls' elementary school, since there weren't enough places for German teachers in her hometown of Laibach, the future Ljubljana. She was a teacher heart and soul and took great pleasure in teaching children, but she found Gottschee itself oppressive. The Gottscheer were a breed apart who spoke their own antiquated variety of German, a centuries-old dialect that automatically kept outsiders at a distance, even when they only came from Laibach, sixty kilometres away.

Carniola's provincial capital seemed a different world. City life. Social gatherings. The Laibach Philharmonic. The German theatre. The German casino. Elaborate balls. Laibach was a Slovenian city, but Germans formed a substantial minority, held important positions in politics and business and were correspondingly self-confident. 'We felt at home in Laibach,' my grandmother told me – the name Ljubljana never crossed her lips, for it would have seemed a betrayal to her – 'Laibach was *our* city, we shopped in *our* shops, went to *our* restaurants, associated with *our* people, with Germans.' My grandmother's father, Josef Lehner, was Laibach's municipal carpenter, another immigrant. He and his wife Magdalena were Danube Swabians, who had migrated from the Hungarian town of Mosony near the Austrian border. Neither of them spoke Slovenian, nor did their daughter, my grandmother. 'We were in contact with Slovenes, yes,' she said, 'but they all spoke German.'

Compared with Laibach, the town of Gottschee was a provincial backwater, just a large village. In 1900 it had a little fewer than 3,000 inhabitants. There was a branch terminal line connecting the place to Laibach, but otherwise it lay off all the major traffic routes. Nevertheless, or perhaps precisely for this reason, the Gottscheer were adept travellers. Since the Middle Ages, men from the *Ländchen*, 'the little province', as they affectionately called their region, had journeyed as pedlars through the provinces of the empire from autumn to spring every year, first with carved goods and linen, and then later with spices and tropical fruits. The inhabitants of the German enclave's widely scattered villages couldn't make their living from agriculture alone. The winters on the limestone karst highlands were long and hard, the soils poor. Every field, every meadow had to be wrested from the forest. The great emigration to America began at the end of the nineteenth century and its effects were already apparent in the town of Gottschee; the place was marked by decline even before the First World War.

Apart from the Auersperg Castle and a few official buildings like the high school and the timber-industry training college, Gottschee had no particular sights to speak of, except perhaps the Rinse, the little river that winds through the town in so broad and picturesque a loop that it surrounds it on three sides. The Rinse is notable for another reason: the sluggish stretch of water (the name is supposedly a contraction of '*rinnender See*', 'flowing

9

lake') arises an hour's walk above the town only to disappear back into the honeycombed karst an hour south of it, as if its task consisted solely in beautifying the settlement nestling in the broad basin of the valley.

My grandmother never really settled into Gottschee. 'A nasty dump and that's that,' she'd say; she was prone to apodictic judgements that brooked no contradiction. In this respect she remained a teacher all her life, although she only practised the profession for a few years. She never told me how she met my grandfather, but it was probably inevitable: both of them were young and single and outsiders in the little town.

My grandfather immediately felt at home there. Sometimes, when he talked about that period of his life, he said he would happily have stayed in Gottschee. He had grown up in a much smaller place and loved, when he looked up from his desk, to be able to let his gaze roam over hills and woods. The town on the Rinse is encircled by wooded ranges that crowd in upon the settlement: to the east the Hornwald Massif, which the Slovenians call Kočevski Rog, to the west the Friedrichsteiner Wald. Grandfather was a passionate hunter, a pastime he could indulge to his heart's content as a young attorney in Gottschee. He had a hunting hut in the Hornwald where he spent days and weeks of his holidays, and continued to do so, even after he had moved to Amstetten, when he was faced with a long, arduous journey to get there.

Why he left Gottschee before the First World War with his wife and child – my father, who was barely a year old – to move to Lower Austria, I cannot say. Perhaps he anticipated the changes that were to lead in 1919 to the formation of the Kingdom of Yugoslavia and to the Germans' resettlement and expulsion from Carniola.

My grandfather often used to tell me about the hunting in Gottschee when I was a child; that was in the late 1940s and early

1950s, in the Traunviertel in Upper Austria and the Mostviertel in Lower Austria. We used to go hiking through the villages, across huge fields of wheat and oats, over meadows of scattered fruit trees that were carpeted with rotting pears, and make our way from farm to farm, where we would find food – potatoes, tender bacon, bread, eggs – and a bed. I remember once thinking I was going to suffocate in a bed because the kindly farmer's wife had tucked me up in two huge eiderdowns, one on top of me and one under the sheet, as was the custom in that part of the countryside. I felt I was sinking into a sack of feathers. The bartered food was probably the point of our trips, although nothing was ever said about it. I had my own little rucksack, which I was tremendously proud of, but the food didn't really interest me very much. All that mattered were the walks with my beloved grandfather, who I called Opsi; the chance to be close to him; the stories of his childhood in Tüffer, of the dormice that made noisy mischief under the roof like tiny, furry hobgoblins, of the peg-driving and other games I didn't know, of the huge Danube salmon he had pulled out of the Sann, the river on which Tüffer stands. And over and over, the tales of hunting in the Gottschee virgin forest with its mighty beeches and oaks, whose girth the arms of two men could not encompass, and its deep karst caves and dolines (I had no real idea what dolines were; the term didn't feature in my vocabulary of the time, I only knew that they were somewhere wild animals could hide) where wounded wild boar and other game lurked so that, just as the hunter came close, they'd burst out of the undergrowth, straight at Opsi – a danger he could only avert with one lightning-fast, unerringly aimed shot. I never saw him shoot – his hunting days were long past by then – but I was convinced of his marksmanship. He used to describe the wolves to me with their greenish, evil, gleaming eyes; how they'd prowl around the log cabin howling with hunger in winter; how growling bears would threaten to break down the door with their massive paws. I can still hear him imitating the howling of the wolves. It would send icy chills up my spine, and then I'd take his hand and we'd march on for hours, kilometre after kilometre, as he told a ceaseless stream of stories in that soft, almost sing-song Lower Styrian dialect that he never lost. Yet he was a tall, thickset man and there was nothing else soft about him; he was choleric and quick-tempered, a rough customer feared by a good many people. But he was always kind to me.

Gottschee and Tüffer were vivid places in the geography of my childhood, more vivid than those in which I grew up, perhaps because, as a result of the Second World War and post-war turmoil, evacuation and flight, I was constantly on the move, first with my mother and then with my grandparents. After our house in Linz was destroyed in an American air raid, I was taken to my grandparents in Amstetten, only for them to flee north again from the advancing Russians a few months later. My grandparents found refuge near Linz, in a place called Oftering, while my mother was evacuated with her three children to Styria, where we stayed until 1948. I travelled on my own from there to Oftering and stayed with my grandfather on a farm, in the farmer's little retirement house. I remember the outside wooden stairs that led up to our room, how they creaked under his weight and how that made us laugh, and my olive-green sleeping bag made out of coarse, scratchy wool. After a few months, the bombed house was rebuilt and I was fetched back to Linz to start school in 1950.

My grandfather's stories of Gottschee and Tüffer comforted me throughout these unsettled years, stories of a world in which everything always remained constant and unchanging, no matter how often one talked about it.

3

Today, maps show Tüffer as the small Slovenian town of Laško in the Štajerska region, twelve kilometres south of Celje in the Savinja Valley. But when my great-grandfather, Paul Bast, immigrated there from the Rhineland it was in Lower Styria, then the southern half of the Habsburg crownland of Styria, and the neighbouring town was called Cilli in the Sann valley. (The official use of Slovenian names dates from the Treaty of Versailles after the First World War, when the entire region came under Yugoslav control.)

My grandfather had always led me to believe that he came from an old Tüffer family that had lived there for centuries. It was only when I began to work on this book that I found out that they were all immigrants. The Rhinelander Paul Bast married Juliane Renier, the daughter of a respected citizen in Tüffer, had eight children with her – or perhaps more; at any rate that was how many survived – and ran a tannery in the small market town that brought him and his family considerable affluence. He built a splendid house directly opposite Tüffer's squat parish church, which is still standing today.

What prompted the Rhinelander to settle in an area in the far south of the Habsburg Empire, with a predominantly Slovene population, and whether he founded the tannery or married into the business is not clear from the comparatively few remaining documents I have been able to find. What emerges clearly, though, is that my great-grandfather was Catholic, like his wife, and a hard-working, personable man who was recognized and respected in Tüffer, with an appointed place at the prominent citizens' regular table, their *Stammtisch*, in the Horiak Hotel. He was several times elected a municipal representative, performed his civic duty as a juror at the Assize Court in Cilli, served as Chairman of the District Savings Bank and captain of the volunteer fire brigade and was a stalwart member of all the nationalist organizations in Tüffer, in particular the town's Beautification Society and the German School Association.

The Germans made up two thirds of Tüffer's population in 1900 and were typical representatives of the provincial middle class: merchants, craftsmen, a few industrialists, the skilled workers at the sawmills on the Sann River, several doctors employed in the sanatorium at the Kaiser Franz Josef Health Spa, the spa's owner, a certain Theodor Gunkel, a notary public, an advocate and a few teachers. Graf Vetter von der Lilie's *schloss*, which he had had built in place of the ruined castle on the hill above the town, stretched imposingly along one bank of the Sann, while the Kaiser Franz Josef Health Spa across the river lent the place an almost elegant, cosmopolitan air. The patients' and guests' registers record a succession of middle-ranking civil servants, gentlemen of independent means, landowners and merchants from all parts of the empire. There was another spa, Römerbad Tüffer, a few kilometres upstream. Densely wooded hills hem in the valley on both sides, their rounded hilltops crowned with white pilgrimage churches, while above the town towers the Hum, a striking cone-shaped mountain that has vines and sweet chestnuts growing on its slopes. Many of Tüffer's inhabitants had fields, vineyards and beehives in the surrounding hills; at the turn of the century the division between the near-urban life of the town and the self-sufficiency of the countryside had yet to become absolute.

The Basts were pillars of Tüffer's German bourgeoisie. The eldest son, Ludwig, a medical student, was a member of the Tüffer *Liedertafel* (Male Voice Choral Society) and a popular speaker and amateur actor. He performed regularly at New Year's Eve parties and similar functions, often alongside his sisters Käthi and Josefine, known as Pepi, two pretty girls full of *joie de vivre* who never missed a single performance of the Tüffer Amateur Dramatics Society.

When the Amateur Dramatics Society put on a one-act play entitled *The Little People* in the hall of the Horiak Hotel, the *German Watch*, the organ of the German nationalists published in Cilli, praised the acting of Fräulein Pepi and Käthi Bast, but went on to deplore the fact that there were Slovenes to be seen among the enthusiastically applauding audience:

> In these times of hard struggle, when the Slavs, partly by open warfare, partly by their notorious sly manoeuvrings, are increasingly forcing their way into our circles, we would have preferred to see a clear separation prevailing at such a fine celebration in Tüffer, and we would have wished that this charity benefit could have remained a purely German event.

Everything in the Styrian lowlands was divided along lines of national affiliation and language: inns and associations, financial institutions and schools, reading rooms, newspapers, wayside shrines, even church services. The Slovenes planted limes along their squares, the Germans oaks. The Slovenes paid their money into the *Posojilnica*, the Germans into the *Sparkasse*. 'Hie Slowenen: Hie Deutsche!' went the slogan ('Slovenes here, Germans there!'). Both sides were obsessed with protecting their language, with preventing any violations of the invisible border, the 'language border'. The Germans called themselves *Sprachgrenzdeutsche*, 'language-border Germans': it had a deliberately belligerent ring to it.

In 1892, through the offices of the German School Association, a German elementary school with four classes was opened in Tüffer, even though the little place already had an elementary school. But that was a bilingual institution, with instruction in Slovenian and German, and the Germans spurned such *utraquistic** schools. Many considered the possibility of German children learning their neighbours' language a threat to their national identity. In Lower Styria, where predominantly German cities and market towns formed joint catchment areas with surrounding Slovenian rural communities, the German School Association, established in 1880 at the suggestion of Englebert Pernerstorfer, later co-founder of the Austrian Social Democratic Party, sought to segregate the two ethnic groups, at least in the classroom, through the creation of purely German schools. The Germans of Tüffer and neighbouring Cilli saw the opening of their own elementary school as an important victory in the holding action against the encroaching Slovenians. The province of Carniola and its capital Laibach stood as a warning: once the southernmost outpost of what the German nationalists called *Deutschtum* – German identity, German culture, *Germanness* – Carniola had been overrun by Slovenes and waited to be recaptured.

'On Sunday we celebrate a red-letter day. A new German schoolhouse has been inaugurated in Markt Tüffer. To those of us who live in the southernmost German March, who are entirely surrounded by Slav-speaking half-breeds, who at every turn see the achievements of our age-old culture endangered and threatened – to us the founding of a further German bulwark must be especially precious,' wrote the *German Watch* at the school's inauguration. This bi-weekly newspaper was read like the Bible in my great-grandfather's house. The major nationalist organizations marched in close formation from Cilli, twelve kilometres away, to celebrate Tüffer's big day: the German Gymnastic Club, the German Cyclists Club, the Cilli Male Voice Choral Society.

---

*Speaking or using both languages, from the Latin *utraque*: 'each' or 'both', as in the phrase *sub utraque specie*: 'under each kind'.

Every organization had its motto. 'A German song on a German tongue / Buoys the heart of a German son,' was the Male Voice Choral Society's slogan. The Cilli cyclists had 'In merry circles / Let "Naught But German" / Be a German cyclist's motto / A German cyclist's bastion' emblazoned on their banner.

The Slovenes, meanwhile, sang and hiked and performed gymnastics in their own clubs. There was a liberal gymnastic club, the *Sokoli*, the Falcons, based on a Czech model, and later even a Christian one, the *Orli*, which the Germans mockingly called *Tschukis* or Owls. The Czechs were held in high regard by Slovene nationalists for their success in standing up to the Germans in the empire. Gymnastic competitions, whichever permutation of German, Slovenian, Christian or liberal clubs they involved, regularly ended in fights and often in bloodshed.

The Bast children were enthusiastic gymnasts, which was itself a form of training in cultural nationalism. My grandfather told me one of Jahn's,* the old 'Father of Gymnastics', sayings: 'Honour the German tongue, defend against the Romance on every front.' I can't remember when he said this; there weren't any people from Romance countries living in Amstetten who might have prompted it, nor any Slovenes, for that matter.

Slovenes and Germans often came to blows with one another over trivialities. If Czech cyclists and gymnasts, the *Sokoli*, visited their Slavic brothers in Cilli (Celje to them), or if farm lads at a fair boisterously shouted '*Živio!*', the equivalent of 'Your good health!', the Germans immediately felt provoked. At first they'd respond with a vigorous '*Heil!*', then the beer mugs and fists would start flying. Educated Slovenes, advocates, doctors, civil servants and vicars, would shout '*Pereat Germania!*' ('May

*Friedrich Ludwig Jahn (1778–1852) founded the *Turnverein* (gymnastic club) movement in Germany during the Napoleonic Wars. A fervent patriot, he believed physical education was the key to restoring German morale and strengthening German national identity after defeat by the French.

Germany Perish!') rather than '*Živio!*' – after all, they had learnt Latin at the German grammar school in Cilli – and then the German graduates would join the fray. Sometimes people were even shot. Police and courts were inundated. The clashes were reported in painstaking detail by the *German Watch*. Naturally the Slovenes were always the instigators, the provocateurs; the Germans had no choice but to defend themselves.

When members of the German Cyclists Club of Cilli went on an outing into the countryside in July 1898, they were met with shouts of '*Živio!*' and showers of stones in the small town of Tüchern. The cyclists were prepared for such incidents; most were carrying loaded revolvers.

A range of fraternities and societies were created for the promotion of *Deutschtum* in the Styrian lowlands, such as the Südmark (Southern March) Association, which saw it as its job to settle German farmers in mixed districts in order to protect endangered land. It concentrated its activities on the hills of the Windische* Büheln (Slovenske gorice in Slovenian), which drew protests from Slovenes in Cilli and the Lower Sann valley. In 1885 German students in Cilli founded the *Germania* Fraternity of German Undergraduates in Lower Styria, which later metamorphosed into the *Germania zu Graz Burschenschaft* (duelling fraternity). The fraternity members regularly travelled from Graz to celebrate their founding anniversary in Cilli and go on day trips to Tüffer and other nearby places where they held nationalist rallies that featured plenty of speechmaking, singing and drinking. 'Hail to Germania, Mother of Us All!' The fraternity members wanted to show solidarity with their German brothers in the lowlands, and they wanted the Slovenes to see it.

*A derivative of '*Wends*', the haphazard, catch-all German name for the Slavic peoples on medieval Germany's eastern borders, '*Winds*' and the adjective '*Windish*' were German terms for the Slovenes and Slovenian, with either neutral or pejorative connotations.

All the Basts who studied in Graz joined the Germania fraternity and fought their student duels there: my grandfather, my father, my uncle. As a child, I thought men had duelling scars in the same way they had a growth of beard.

There's a photo of my father walking, no, marching towards the photographer with a grim expression on his face, a cane in his right hand, a briefcase jammed under his left arm. Even though it's winter, and there's snow in the background, he is wearing a light trench coat. He has a close-fitting black cap on his head and bandages over both cheeks, which are probably tied together over his head and held in place by the cap. On the back of the photograph he has written in his Gothic script, 'This is what "*hors de combat*" looks like.' The picture presumably dates from his student days in Graz.

Another, older picture shows a slim young man in full fraternity

regalia, with a plumed toque on his head, a sash across his chest, turned-up boots and light, tight trousers. My grandfather. The picture comes from a *Germania zu Graz* brochure and bears the caption 'Rudolf Bast as X' in block capitals. X signifies Senior or head of the fraternity (Speaker and *Erster Chargierter* are other names for the position), even though my grandfather looks extremely young in the photo. He had enrolled in Graz's Law Faculty in the winter term of 1900 and joined the Germania fraternity shortly thereafter. In 1902 he became Germania's Fencing Guardian, and in the summer of 1903 its Senior, which meant both

running the fraternity and being its public face. He was particularly passionate about their so-called 'borderlands work', which regularly took him to Lower Styria, to Marburg, Cilli and Laibach. In the photograph he is leaning against a table, propping his hands in their white turned-up gloves on a basket-hilt *Schläger*, the broadsword used for student duels.

The spell cast by weapons on our family, particularly guns. Hunting guns, shooting rifles, combination over-and-under rifles and shotguns, revolvers. Guns were always being talked about; even old ones, owned in the past, continued to be spoken of like dearly departed family members. 'My Mannlicher-Schönauer, my Sauer-Stutzen,' grandfather would say, sorrow and rage in his voice. As the Russians approached in 1945, he had carefully wrapped his hunting rifles in oiled cloths and tarpaulins and buried them, but had then been unable to find the place when he returned to Amstetten five years later. Perhaps someone had dug them up. *His* guns.

When, back in the first decade of the century, Slovenes insisted on equal rights for their language and demanded bilingual street signs in Cilli and Marburg, the two biggest towns in the lowlands, they were cursed as 'Windish agitators' or '*Pervaken*'.* The response was similar if they spoke in their own language in a German pub in Cilli or Tüffer; the regulars put a stop to such '*pervakische*' pushiness in forthright, often violent ways. People tried to enforce the division between the two groups in shops as well, to support their kind and undermine their adversaries. 'Germans, buy from Germans!' preached the *German Watch*. '*Svoji k svojim!*' ('Each to his own!') the cry echoed back from the Slovene side.

---

*A German form of '*prvaki*', the name Slovenian liberals gave their conservative counterparts to mock what they thought of as their tendency to act as if they were the first, '*prvi*', the masters.

From a present-day perspective, these disputes and struggles seem laughable stuff: petty squabbles, drunken affairs, bar-room brawls masquerading as great nationalist battles. But on closer inspection, something was announcing itself here that a few decades later would be carried out in deadly earnest and with murderous perfection: the displacement, expulsion and, ultimately, eradication of the foreigners, the others, the Jews, the Slavs, the Slovenes. Even at the time, some conflicts already had an impact far beyond the borders of Lower Styria, notably the dispute over Cilli's Gymnasium (grammar school), which reverberated through the entire Habsburg Empire.

It began with reports in Slovene newspapers that German pupils at Cilli Gymnasium, 'the callow descendants of red-haired Teutons', were holding secret meetings in which they bedecked the pictures of Bismarck and the German Emperor with garlands, sang anti-Austrian songs and shouted, 'Long live Bismarck! Long live Germany!' This was sensational, insurrectionary behaviour. Slovene deputies to the Viennese parliament immediately tabled demands for the Gymnasium to introduce parallel classes in Slovenian. Cilli's German inhabitants indignantly rejected this as infringing their vested rights and endangering *Deutschtum* in the lowlands. The struggle for the school swung back and forth for months and was finally ended by the creation in Cilli of a Slovenian Untergymnasium, a lower school with two classes preparing students for the Gymnasium, which in turn led to the fall of the Viennese coalition government of the Prime Minister, Prince zu Windischgrätz, in 1895, when infuriated German members of parliament refused to approve his budget.

The Cilli controversy not only brought down the government, but also permanently poisoned the atmosphere in Lower Styria. My grandfather, who was born in 1880, was a pupil of the grammar school at the time. He was going on fifteen and enthusiastically adopted the fighting talk of the older generation. The fight for the school was their 'Watch on the Sann'. The Slovenes wanted to bring them to their knees. Lower Styria was a theatre of war in which Germans had to defend themselves to the last drop of their blood.

Things were not always so belligerent in everyday life; despite the chauvinistic slogans, many Slovenes and Germans associated with one another socially as well as in business. In predominantly German Cilli, the Slovenes had no choice but to shop at German establishments, the Germans having the town's business well in hand. Similarly, the German tanner Paul Bast employed Slovene servants in his house in Tüffer, Slovene workers in his tannery and, if the price was right, he bought hides from Slovene dealers. Slovenes and Germans lived side by side. The geographer and historian Fran Orožen, the first president of the Slovene Alpine Society, was born in the house next to my great-grandfather in 1853, an event which is commemorated today by a plaque. There were mixed marriages and friendships, even among obsessive German nationalists and fanatical Slovenes, even between the wars and afterwards. This was possible between friends and relatives; they could forget the ideology and the radical talk for a while and sit down together to eat and drink and enjoy themselves. But social life did not really change people. They remained true to their convictions and simply removed them for a little while like a coat that they checked in at a cloakroom and then put on again when they went outside. Outside, where Germans and Slovenes beat each other's brains out.

The Germans in the lowlands saw themselves as a bulwark against the Slavic tide, discriminated against and betrayed on all sides, by the government in Vienna as much as by the Catholic Church, which filled every vacancy in its clergy with 'rabble-rousing Slovenian parsons'. The *German Watch* proffered countless examples of the perfidy of radical Slovene priests, purportedly stirring up the good-natured Slovenian country folk against the

Germans. These growing tensions paved the way for ideologues like the rabid German nationalist Georg Schönerer* and his 'Away from Rome' movement. 'To be German means to be free of Rome. Without Judas, without Rome, we shall build God's German Home.' The *German Watch* carried instructions on how to convert from the Catholic faith to Protestantism, the 'natural German religion'. One of the increasingly popular Protestant hymns began, 'Luther goes through every nation / Praise ye, his German land and congregation.'

The great majority of Germans in Lower Styria remained true to the Catholic Church, but Schönerer's pan-German followers gained ground among the intellectuals and students. Anti-Habsburg and anti-clerical Germans also adopted Schönerer's use of '*Heil*', the German greeting, and his aggressive anti-Semitism; Adolf Hitler, who was inspired by Schönerer, was one of them.

The Basts also slowly turned away from the Catholic Church over its dealings with the Slovenes. I am not sure whether the tanner himself converted; his son Rudolf, my grandfather, was still baptized a Catholic. But as early as 1910 Rudolf was married in the Protestant church in Laibach and later he served for many years as trustee of the Protestant parish in Amstetten.

Rather than the otherwise omnipresent Emperor Franz Josef, it was the Prussian Wilhelm, with his piercing gaze and boldly twirled moustache, whose portrait hung in the Basts' parlour in Tüffer, although as a Rhinelander Paul Bast didn't as a rule much care for Prussians. But he cared for them more than for the Habsburgs, who were traitors, friends of the Slav, the Czechs, the Slovenes. All the family's hopes rested on Germany: the German

*Georg Ritter von Schönerer (1842–1921), founder of the Austrian Pan-German Party in 1885, a virulent anti-Semite and German nationalist who had a broad following among the antidemocratic Viennese lower middle class and the student fraternities.

Reich and the Iron Chancellor, Bismarck. 'We Germans fear God up above, but nothing else in this world.' 'The God that makes the iron grow.'

On Sundays the family went on outings, mostly into the countryside around Tüffer. Sometimes they took the Southern Railway to Cilli and walked to the Bismarck Hill, where they met others of like mind. Adolescents and children wore cornflowers – Kaiser Wilhelm's favourite flower, the badge of the German nationalists – in their jackets and caps. On their way home 'The Watch on the Rhine' and other nationalist songs were sung. On 1 April 1895 Bismarck's eightieth birthday was enthusiastically celebrated in all the German towns in Lower Styria. Julie Horiak's restaurant in Tüffer was packed; the room was adorned with a picture of the 'Blacksmith of the German Reich' at his anvil as he forged the sword of Germania, a popular motif disseminated in thousands of cheap prints and postcards. The men proposed rousing toasts and the Southern Styrian sparkling wine flowed like water. The next day Tüffer's Bismarck admirers sent their congratulations to the German Chancellor in his retirement residence in Friedrichsruh.

Otherwise life in Tüffer took a more humdrum course. Paul Bast had many worries: the tannery wasn't doing as well as it had done initially; the competition from larger businesses gave him trouble. That was the way of things: there had been seven tanneries in Cilli in 1800; by the second half of the nineteenth century there were only three left. One day Bast opened an inn on the ground floor of his house as something to fall back on; the family still had plenty of room. Shortly after the turn of the century his eldest daughter, Anna, married the land agent Wilhelm Edler von Eckhel. In the same year Rudolf Bast passed the *Matura* (the school-leaving examination). He was twenty, which would suggest that he had repeated a year or two, but grandfather never talked about it. School wasn't one of his passions; only fishing and hunting. One of his school reports shows that Cilli's Gymnasium was attended by 190 Germans, sixty-nine Slovenes and two Czechs. Two hundred and fifty-three pupils were Catholic, seven were Protestant and the institution contained one Jew. In addition to which 119 pupils, presumably all of Slovene origin, attended 'independent Gymnasium classes with instruction in German and Slovenian'. So Slovenes sent their children to the German school, as before, but not the other way round.

My grandfather hadn't properly settled in as a student in Graz when his father Paul Bast died unexpectedly of a heart attack in February 1901, aged fifty-six. The Tüffer fire brigade gave their captain a 'pack farewell', a traditional fraternity send-off, in the Horiak Hotel. The new captain gave a memorial address and then the firemen 'rubbed a salamander in mourning', which meant they scraped their beer mugs on the tables and drank a toast to the deceased. In the obituary in the *German Watch*, the master tanner and landlord was honoured as a staunch German who had given devoted service to all Tüffer's nationalist associations. Particular emphasis was laid on his contribution to the reorganization of the town's cemetery.

4

A rectangular black marble plaque with twelve names, one of which is Franc Drolc, born 28.3.1873, died 9.3.1962. The gravestone in the new part of Laško's (once Tüffer's) cemetery has been pointed out to us by an old woman with a crutch who is clearing wilted flowers from a grave. I have entered the name in my notebook. Franc Drolc was the sacristan, organist and choirmaster of Laško, and was married to Pauline Bast, a daughter of the tanner Paul Bast.

The lives of the tanner's children map this region's turbulent history during the first decades of the twentieth century. His four sons went to Austria, three of his daughters ended up in Zagreb and only one, Pauline, stayed with her mother in Tüffer. After Paul Bast's death, mother and daughter tried to run the tannery with a journeyman, but he was more interested in lining his own pockets than helping two women with no experience in business. They then tried their luck with the inn on the ground floor of their house, but that was no more successful. At some point between the wars Pauline Bast (long since an old maid by the standards of the time) married the Slovenian sacristan Franc Drolc. His gravestone bears the names of his first wife, Franja, who died in 1919, and of the five children they had together. The youngest, Dušan, was killed fighting for the partisans against the Germans in 1942; Ana, the last to die, was buried in 2001. 'A beautiful funeral,' the woman with the crutch says. 'Now there's no one from the family living here any more.' Drolc's second wife, Pauline, was presumably buried in the Basts' grave, which we have yet to find.

It is a clear September day; only a single cloud hangs motionless over the green cone of Mount Hum. I have come to Laško with my wife to look for the Basts' house and any other traces of the family we can find. She knows the place from childhood; her grandfather in Ljubljana used to spend a few weeks every year at the Laško Health Spa to treat the persistent effects of a wound he had picked up in the First World War. He had a stiff knee and his lower leg, which had never properly healed, had to be freshly dressed every day. It always felt like an adventure to her, every time she went to visit her grandfather – who she called Ata – in Laško.

The hills covered with deciduous trees on either side of the Sann have begun to change colour. The graveyard lies in the afternoon sun; tiny brown lizards scurry over the gravestones. I remember that these nimble animals are called *martinček* in Slovenian, 'little Martins'.

The graveyard visitor with the crutch has been watching my wife and me for quite a while as we read the inscriptions and wander between the graves before she finally brings herself to talk to us. The Basts' grave? 'That was somewhere over there before,' she says, gesturing vaguely with her hand towards the graves in the old part of the graveyard. A wall with two openings divides the old section from the new. The oldest graves lie along the outer wall: Johann Drofenik, Forwarding Clerk, Southern Railways, 1818–1888. Eng. Adolf Widra, Mine Director 1855–1931. Henke Franc, Hotelier, 1888–1940. Franc Henke took over the German associations' favourite meeting place, the Horiak Hotel, which later bore his name. A massive grey headstone is inscribed Rodbina Dergan, Dergan Family. 'Merchants,' the old woman explains. 'Everyone knew them round here.' The name is familiar. In my father's journal, the slim little book that was found on his body and turned over to my grandmother, the name Laško is written in pencil on the last page and underneath: Perdich Emil – Butcher; Pleskovič Emil – Tax Office Dir.; I.R., Dergan – Merchant.

I imagine he jotted down the names when he was on the run, look-ing for somewhere to hide after the collapse of the Thousand-Year Reich that in Austria lasted barely eight years.

It is hard to understand why he wrote 'Laško', the Slovenian name for the place, rather than 'Tüffer', or what the three names – perhaps family acquaintances – mean exactly. The Dergan head-stone bears the names of three men: Rudolf, 1886–1947, the mer-chant, and his two sons, Branko and Boris (no longer alive by then, having died in 1937 at the age of nineteen). Was my father a friend of Branko, who was roughly the same age as him, or was there a connection with their father? Was he hoping to get in touch with these Slovenian acquaintances or friends? Did he expect them to find him a hiding place, false papers, money? I don't know and, since the protagonists are all dead, I will probably never find out.

We find graves with the names Perdich and Pleskovič, but no Bast, only Drolc, who married Pauline Bast. The Bast children called him 'Uncle Drolc', as he did himself, as if he had no first name. I only learnt it from his gravestone. He signed letters and cards to relatives with a brief and to-the-point 'Drolc', or, if they were children, 'Uncle Drolc'. He was a popular uncle. When rela-tives visited Laško, he showed the children how to make com-munion wafers with a special iron, which was part of his duties as sacristan, and when he played the organ he took them up into the gallery with him and allowed them to work the pedals.

The Basts retained links with Laško through all the political changes and upheavals. The tanner's children regularly met up in the years between the wars at the family house in Tüffer, which by then was in Yugoslavia and officially just called Laško. Aunt Pauline cooked for everybody, and they went on outings to the surrounding countryside, to Römerbad or the Hum or St Christoph mountains, where the Germans had lit their solstice fires before 1918. When his various duties allowed him, Uncle Drolc went along too.

The organist and sacristan was a well-known figure in Laško, a highly respected man. '*Gospod* organist Drolc,' the woman with the crutch says reverentially when she talks about him. She knew him well; her father sang in the church choir when Drolc was choirmaster. Later she shows us a picture of him: a dignified man with a goatee beard, sitting self-assuredly among a group of men and women in their Sunday best who are looking slightly shyly into the camera: Laško's mixed church choir. She has another picture of herself as a young girl amid a cluster of other girls the same age, some of whom are wearing a sort of uniform: white blouse, knotted scarf and dark skirt. 'Hitler Youth,' she says laughing, as if she has happy memories of that time. There are only girls in the picture. In April 1941 former Lower Styria was occupied by Nazi Germany and annexed to the *Reichsgau* Styria. Tens of thousands of Slovenes were resettled; those that resisted ended up in concentration camps or were murdered. Uncle Drolc's only son joined the partisans.

It is not recorded how Uncle Drolc fared during the German occupation. His marriage to a German woman presumably afforded him some protection, even though he was considered a Slovenian troublemaker in German circles. Before the First World War he had, in addition to his positions in Tüffer's church, been municipal council secretary of Marija Gradec (Maria Graz in German), the nearby pilgrimage place, which led German residents to call him a 'Windish council agitator'. Drolc knew Slovenes' legal rights and he refused to be browbeaten. But these frictions with German nationalists did not prevent him later marrying a German and moving into her house – the Basts' family house. 'It was a *German* house,' grandfather would say when he reminisced about Tüffer.

The woman with the crutch who knew Drolc well shows us the house. It stands at the bottom of Laško's steeply sloping church square, opposite the *Mariensäule* (the column of the Virgin

Mary), a huge grey-painted structure consisting of a one-storey, L-shaped main house and a ground-level extension that presumably housed the tannery. Everything has been newly renovated. There are curtains in some of the windows, but still the house gives the impression of being unoccupied. The entrance gate is locked, as is a side gate leading to a narrow interior courtyard. Our guide cannot say who the house belongs to now. The break-up of the Yugoslav state has left a complicated tangle of restitution claims in Slovenia, which first have to be slowly unravelled. After the death of Pauline, who remained childless, the house passed to Uncle Drolc, who in turn gave it to his daughter from his first marriage. And thus, as the Amstetten relatives who bear Drolc a grudge even in death would say, the tanner Paul Bast's house, a stronghold of *Deutschtum*, ended up falling into Slovenian hands. A piece of malice on history's part or an instance of poetic justice, depending on one's point of view.

Gospod organist Drolc and Pauline Bast. How complicated national relations could be in Lower Styria at the turn of the nineteenth into the twentieth century can be seen from the fact that in little Tüffer, which had just under 800 inhabitants in 1893, there also lived a staunchly German nationalist family by the name of Drolz (with a 'z' rather than a 'c'). When the Südmark Association set up a branch in Tüffer in October 1899 to extend the fight against Slovenian equality, municipal councillor Josef Drolz delivered a withering attack on 'Windish commerce'. He concluded his speech with the trenchant declaration, 'Tüffer is and will always be a German town!'

Uncle Drolc was sixteen at the time and, one would assume, related to the German municipal councillor Josef Drolz. The dividing lines often ran through families: one part 'Slovenized' itself, while the other upheld its *Deutschtum* and were enemies of the Slovenes. But instances of peaceable coexistence can be found even in the Bast household.

As we are rummaging through a box of old photos of Laško in Celje's main library, my wife discovers two postcards sent from Laško to Josefine Bast's family in Zagreb. One is a birthday card to Josefine's daughter Klara from her Aunt Pauline and her Uncle Drolc. Pauline writes in German and her husband underneath in Slovenian. The card is postmarked 1930. The two practise genuine bilingualism under one roof. The second card is from Klara's brother Guido, who evidently spent a few days with his relatives in Laško, to his mother in Zagreb. He writes in German, although not without mistakes.

Dear Mama, I'm recovering visually [*sic*]. Almost every day I get up at 12 because the air makes me sleepy. Already there isn't quite enough snow left to sky [*sic*]. Uncle Drolc is busy choosing nuts for a nut strudel. Regards from Aunt Paula and Drolc, Your Guido.

The card is undated, the postmark illegible.

In a photo I found in my father's belongings, Guido is standing in front of a house, perhaps the Basts'. He is wearing a dark, heavy cloth coat, a scarf and tie. A centre parting, slightly skewed to the left, divides his dark, wavy hair. He is smiling quizzically, his eyes screwed up as if he is looking into the sun. 'Laško 1940, Guido a little hung over,' it says on the back in my father's handwriting. A second picture, probably taken at the same time, shows my grandfather lying in bed, a quilt pulled up to his chin, smiling somewhat forcedly. 'Laško 1940,' my father has written on the back. 'Effects of the parting cup.'

So the relatives from Amstetten and Zagreb also met up in Laško in 1940, when the war had been going on for a year. The following year German troops would march into Yugoslavia. They would occupy Laško; Slovenes would be expelled, deported and murdered. The family reunion must have taken place at the Bast family house, at Pauline and Drolc's. It is not recorded whether

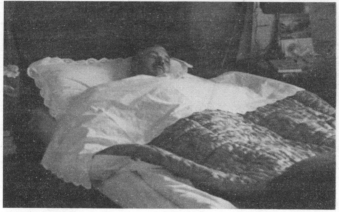

Pauline baked a nut strudel to celebrate; what is certain is that the Amstetten branch of the family knew that Guido was half Jewish. Aunt Josefine had married a Jewish man in Zagreb, who had died young. At the time of the reunion in 1940, my father was a Gestapo officer in Graz. On 1 December 1939 he had been promoted to SS Hauptsturmführer (Captain) and three months later he had been appointed SS liaison to SD Main Office in Berlin (SD was an abbreviation for the *Sicherheitsdienst*, the Security Service of the SS). Soon after that he was transferred to the Graz Gestapo, as head of Abteilung (Department) II, Enemy Investigation and Combat, and from there was able to join the family in Laško. Perhaps they celebrated my grandfather's sixtieth birthday, which was on 21 April 1940. My grandfather in Laško, the parting cup, Guido hung over, the thick coat: that could all fit. Or did this meeting – which is only documented by the two photographs – take place earlier? On 20 April 1940, the Führer's birthday, my grandfather received the NSDAP Bronze Long Service Medal. I don't know whether there was a ceremony that he had to attend in person on the day or whether he could have picked up the award informally from his local party office.

Either way, at some point in 1940 they all sat down together in the family house in Tüffer: Uncle Drolc, the 'Windish council agitator', the Amstetten National Socialists – my grandfather and father had both joined the party in 1931 – and Guido, who, according to their race laws, was less than fully human. And they all drank and were full of good cheer.

5

The road from Laško to Ljubljana runs through the narrow, dark Sava valley, past black factory plants that lie untidily along the river as if washed up by chance, flotsam of an earlier industrialized age. Before Ljubljana the countryside opens out into a plain. An endless line of cars streams out of the city towards us; it's the afternoon, knocking-off time, offices are closing; it looks as if the whole city is in flight. We look out to see where everybody is going: there is no sign of any new housing estates, just villages to the left and right, interspersed with industrial estates and petrol stations.

We are staying in the south of Ljubljana, in the Vič quarter, with our friend Meta Hočevar, a set designer, director and architect. She lives in a quiet cul-de-sac of narrow detached houses with oddly pointed roofs and small gardens. The house opposite belonged to my wife Gridi's grandparents, Jože and Franciska (Franja) Pajntar; Gridi often spent her holidays there, while Meta grew up in the same house she lives in now. Born in 1880, like my grandfather, Jože Pajntar returned from the First World War an invalid, 80 per cent disabled. He started a carpenters' co-operative, was active in the union, went round collecting dues despite his stiff leg and discussed politics in the pub over a glass of red wine. His wife Franja was critical of this passion for politics. It made her feel ashamed to hear members of the middle class call her husband an agitator; once someone even emptied a chamber pot over him. 'If it wasn't for his politics we could have made a nice life for ourselves,' she often said. After Jože died, she lived with Gridi's mother in Vienna for years, without ever learning

German. I got to meet the Stara Mama, as she was known in the family, before she died in Ljubljana aged ninety-seven. Even in old age, she was a tall, beautiful woman. We visited her shortly before her death; she lay in bed and could hardly talk any more, but a smile spread over her gaunt face when my wife took her hand.

As a journeyman carpenter, Jože Pajntar travelled all over the Austro-Hungarian Empire, including the South Tyrol, and later worked for several years in Graz, where he took his master crafts-man's qualifying examination. This was soon after the turn of the century, roughly the same time my Tüffer grandfather was study-ing law in Graz, at Karl-Franzens University, and active in the Germania fraternity. In 1903 my grandfather volunteered for the K. u. k. Albert 1, King of Belgium, Nr. 27 Infantry Regiment, whose men were known for short as Belgians. He served for a year, resumed his law studies in 1904 and graduated in 1907 with the degree of Doctor Juris. That same year he moved to Gottschee.

The staggering proximity of everything. My grandmother grew up in Laibach in Trieste Strasse (Tržaska in Slovenian), at number 8. Her father, the carpenter Josef Lehner, had a comfortable flat in the building, which he also used as an office. The broad arterial road leading out to Trieste still has the same name, but the build-ing has since been pulled down and a block of flats put up in its place. My wife's grandparents' house is barely a stone's throw away, and the old state tobacco factory, the *Tobačna tovarna*, where Franja Pajntar once worked, is next to it, a long brick building set back a house's depth from Tržaska.

For many years Josef Lehner ran the carpentry business of the Carniolan Construction Company in Laibach. On 27 April 1895 an advertisement appeared in the *Laibacher Zeitung* announcing that the master carpenter and officially accredited expert Josef Lehner had set up for himself and opened his own firm. 'All work completed at the most reasonable rates and to the soundest standards; plans and estimates for durable and temporary wooden structures available on demand.' It was an opportune moment. On Easter night 1895 Laibach was struck by a devastating earthquake, which destroyed more than a quarter of the houses in the city of 30,000 inhabitants and rendered more than half uninhabitable. Architects, civil engineers, master builders and carpenters flocked from all parts of the Habsburg Empire to Carniola's provincial capital. Construction companies from Vienna, Prague, Budapest and Zagreb opened branches; the most prestigious took rooms in the elegant Elephant (later Slon) Hotel. Barracks were urgently needed, emergency accommodation for the thousands of people left without a roof over their head and for the many businesses and offices whose premises had been destroyed. Laibach's mayor, Peter Grasselli, placed adverts in all the major newspapers of the crownlands announcing that Laibach was looking for bricklayers, plasterers and carpenters to help rebuild the city, and that they would find work for years to come.

Josef Lehner designed roof trusses, put up barracks and saw his business flourish. The office moved from the flat in Trieste Strasse to an elegant town house in Wiener Strasse, opposite the popular Pri Figovicu restaurant, which is still there today. The family moved into a house, a villa, with a beautiful garden. 'We had *gottvolle Blumen*, divine flowers,' my grandmother used to say. She liked using the old-fashioned-sounding word '*gottvoll*', which I have never heard anyone else use, as if it was reserved for her exclusively.

A photograph shows part of their garden: a gravel path, flowers and bushes in blossom, tall grass. My father stands on the gravel path: a small young boy with longish hair in a striped smock and an apron. In one hand he holds a sprig in flower, in the other a piece of string with which he pulls a little wooden cart. Grandmother, who is a young woman, is coming into the picture from the knee-high grass on the left; the photographer has

cropped off some of her body. 'In the garden in Laibach 1913, before we go to Amstetten,' she has written in delicate Gothic script on the back. From other pictures – often photographs are the only source I have in trying to piece together the past, and they have come to me loose and unsorted – I know that my grandmother spent some time in Laibach again the following year, 1914, the war year. A sepia photograph in an unusually long and thin format shows my father wearing the same smock and apron but already with short hair, clasping a rifle as big as himself in his left hand. A proper air rifle, capable of killing birds and squirrels. He smiles into the camera, his chin proudly thrust forward, a characteristic pose which I recognize from other, later pictures. 'My first proper rifle.' He was given it when he was three years old.

The spell cast by guns. Habits formed at such an early age. Who has bought the three-year-old the big rifle he is showing off so proudly the year the world war began? It can't have been Josef Lehner, since he was no longer alive. The successful company

owner and municipal carpenter of Laibach had died unexpectedly of a heart attack in 1907, aged fifty-nine. Just like the tanner
in Tüffer, who died at the age of fifty-six.

A year after the death of her father, in 1908, having obtained
her teaching diploma, my grandmother was sent to Gottschee's
Girls' Elementary School. Presumably her father's early death had
something to do with her decision to take up a profession. In
Gottschee she met my grandfather, who was working as a trainee
in the practice of a certain Dr Franz Golf, having previously been
articled to a notary in an even smaller place between Marburg
and Cilli. The typical first steps of a provincial attorney's career.
Around this time, convinced by the pan-German, anti-clerical
rhetoric of Schönerer's 'Away from Rome' movement, my grand-

father left the Catholic Church and became a Protestant. He may also have been influenced by Pastor Hegemann, a militant Protestant and radical German nationalist who officiated in Laibach and often went to Gottschee to preach there. These were troubled years in the otherwise peaceful *Ländchen* of Gottschee. Christian Socialists and Liberals had fallen out irreparably. It wasn't unusual for anti-clericals to subject Gottschee's Catholic priest to a late night tin-kettle serenade or even to smash his windows. I can well imagine my grandfather taking part in these activities. He was always fond of rough horseplay, although of course he had to be careful about his reputation in that small town.

In April 1910 he married the twenty-two-year-old Paula Lehner. The marriage was held in the modest Lutheran church in Laibach, which was built in the 1850s and is today, by a sly piece of historical irony, named after the founder of the Slovenian language and literature, Primož Truber, who translated the Gospels and other books of the Bible into the language of the people. Ten months after the wedding, my father was born in Gottschee.

Huge, dark-stained wooden figures mark the approach to a long, clapboard building: mysterious forms, witches' trees, fabulous beasts. In our search for grandfather's Gottschee hunting hut we have come to a lumber firm a little way out of Kočevje which, appropriately for the black sculptures, is called Grča – roughly the Slovenian for the gnarls of a tree. Grča manages large parts of the Kočevski Rog, the Gottscheer Hornwald, and exports its timber all over the world. No one at Grča knows anything about an old hunting hut in the forest that belonged to, or was leased by, an Austrian attorney until the late 1930s.

I am not clear myself why it is so important to me to find the hunting hut or at least the place where it stood. Is it a tribute to my beloved grandfather, who I later blocked out of my mind? An inadequate attempt after so many years – he died in 1960 – to feel close to him again? I suddenly remember the wolf skin he gave me when I was still very small. At first I was a little afraid of the head with its gaping jaws, yellowish teeth, red plaster tongue and cold glass eyes. Grandfather told me that he had shot it in Gottschee and imitated the howling of the wolves. I took the Gottscheer wolf with me when I went to boarding school. Grandmother impressed upon me the necessity of brushing the pelt regularly to stop moths getting at it and she gave me a special brush, on the back of which she had written WOLF in block capitals in indelible pencil, so that I wouldn't mistakenly use it to polish my shoes. There wasn't much danger of that; I can't remember ever polishing my shoes at that school.

One of the people working for Grča tells us about an old forester who knows every corner of the Hornwald, all the dilapidated, rotting huts that are slowly sinking back into the ground, overgrown by the virgin forest, but the man can't be found. I produce a few photographs of the hunting hut, which show a simple, roughly worked log cabin. A hatch over the door leads to an attic, which was presumably where my grandfather slept, and a crooked flue next to the hatch indicates he had a stove, or at least a fireplace, to cook on and to heat the hut; it can get bitterly cold at night in the forest. To the right of the door there is a strikingly shaped rock that was used as a bench. In one of the photographs, my grandfather is sitting on the rock, looking out at the landscape, with three rifles hanging on the wall behind him. Another photograph shows the hut from a distance, on the rounded top of a gentle hill, set in a clearing among tall, slender deciduous trees (young beeches, oaks?). 'Krennbichl hunting hut (Gottschee). August 1933' is written on the back. My father went hunting that year as well. The Grča employee, a delicately built man who has invited us into his office for coffee, shows us a hill called the Kren on a detailed map of the forest. It is 613 metres high and around

six kilometres northeast of Kočevje, not far from the road that cuts through the Hornwald to Kočevske Poljane (as the village of Pöllandl is called today). I later find the name Krenbüchel on an old German map. The man warns us against bears, of which there are many in the forest; they are still active in September, and not animals you want to trifle with.

A gravel road, potholed and rutted from the torrents that race over it after thunderstorms and turn it into a stream-bed, leads into the Gottschee forest. Massive trees – beeches, pines, oaks and maple; at the foot of them glimmering boulders of whitish limestone, flecked with green moss and lichen; a thick, brown layer of leaves uniformly covering the ground. Large areas of the virgin forest have only recently become accessible, having been military prohibited zones since 1945, and they are still shrouded in dark rumours as to what went on in them. A roughly hewn wooden sculpture by the roadside, the first of Christ's Stations of the Cross, is followed by another every hundred metres, until we reach a weathered wooden sign pointing into the thick undergrowth. *Grobisce Pod Krenom*. The Kren Grave. A path leads to a deep doline, which is pitted with holes in the forest floor, the entrances to a karst cave. A brick memorial, like a modern chapel, has been built on the edge of it; there are wooden crosses and candles everywhere under the trees. A second memorial, a sphere of black polished stone, reads: 'Here lie thousands of soldiers of the Slovenian National Army who were murdered by the Communists in June 1945.' I remember grandfather's stories of the deep dolines he used to explore when he was hunting in the Hornwald, the wild boars and bears that would burst out of them when he got close. The first doline I come upon in the Gottschee forest is a mass grave.

When in spring 1945 the soldiers of the German Wehrmacht fled before Tito's partisans from Slovenian territory to Carinthia in Austria, they were joined by tens of thousands of their local allies and opponents of the Communists – Serbian Chetniks, Croatian Ustase, Slovenian Domobranci,* many of whom were trying to escape with their families. The fugitives were disarmed by British troops and handed back to the partisans, who dealt pitilessly with them, irrespective of whether they had blood on their hands or not. 'The hand of justice, the avenging hand of our people has already found most of the traitors harboured by our state and each of our peoples,' Marshal Tito told the cheering crowds in liberated Ljubljana in May 1945. 'Only a small minority of traitors have managed to flee our country.'

---

*The Chetniks were a loose resistance movement that formed after the Nazi invasion of Yugoslavia in 1941, some of whose groups were more anti-Communist than anti-Nazi. The Ustase was the Croatian fascist organization that ran the Independent State of Croatia from 1941–45. The Domobranci were the anti-Communist Slovenian Home Guard.

Tito's nebulous paraphrase was in reality a bloody campaign of revenge wrought by the victors that had little to do with justice. Crammed into buses and trucks, the prisoners were taken to the Hornwald and shot without trial. The bodies were flung into the deep karst caves, where they still lie today; recovery was rarely possible, and most of the victims' names are unknown. No one can say exactly how many people were killed in the Gottscheer Hornwald. 'About 14,000 people, women and children among them, were pitched into the terrible abyss of the Kočevski Rog,' the Slovenian poet Drago Jančar wrote in an essay on totalitarianism in Slovenia.

The forest beyond the mass grave appears untouched. Impenetrable undergrowth and raspberry and blackberry bushes force us into detours; ferns and mushrooms sprout from fallen trees. We come upon another doline ringed with rocks as tall as a man; it does not open on to a karst cave, and so lacks a perimeter of crosses and candles. The partisans knew the forest intimately; they used it as a secure place of retreat and set up strongpoints throughout, some even with hospitals. Looking out for the strikingly shaped rock that was next to the hunting hut, we work our way up to the top of the Kren. We compare rock formations with the photograph. It is unlikely that the hut is still standing – why should a log cabin, of all things, have survived when the forest has swallowed up whole villages? – but the rock ought to be recognizable. The top of the hill, however, is entirely planted with young spruces, their trunks set so closely that it's almost impossible to get through. We find no trace of the hut or the rock bench.

Back on the road we meet two forestry workers. One, a thickset old man in a T-shirt full of holes, asks whether we have someone buried on Kren. The younger one says nothing and just stares mournfully ahead. The old man tells us that he saw the men being brought to the forest in buses and shot where we are standing, just by the road. Everything around was red with blood. 'I was fifteen at the time,' he says, 'and I was with my father in the forest. We were collecting firewood. When the buses came, we hid. If the soldiers had seen us, it'd have been us too . . .' He draws the side of his hand across his throat.

On our way out of the forest, we pass through villages that only exist as names on old maps: no houses, no churches, no grave-yards, only trees, bushes, a clearing in which a church perhaps once stood; an inconspicuous elevation that might indicate the sunken, overgrown remains of a wall. The houses have been pulled down; the bricks used as building material or paving. A waterlogged depression in a meadow may have been a pond in which children swam and women washed clothes. All that people had wrested from it through hard labour the forest has now reclaimed: the villages, the fields, the graves and the hunting hut on Krenbichel.

6

In June 1912 my grandfather left Gottschee with his wife and child and moved to Amstetten in Lower Austria. It's impossible to tell now why he chose that town in particular. Part of it, I suppose, was the fact that Amstetten was a small place and he couldn't find any pleasure in big city life. Even Graz was too large for him. Professionally it would have been more natural for him to set himself up there, in Styria's provincial capital, where he had studied. As a Lower Styrian and member of the Germania fraternity, he had no shortage of friends and acquaintances in Graz from similar backgrounds and with similar nationalist views. Connections mean a great deal to a young attorney. Cilli and Tüffer were also just a few hours from Graz by the Southern Railway, whereas they were an exhausting journey from Amstetten. With the move, the family house in Tüffer and the hunting hut on Krenbichel suddenly receded into the far distance.

It may be that in those years Amstetten was simply an easier place in which to make a life for himself. At the turn of the century the main town in western Lower Austria was gripped by a heady sense of change: there was building everywhere, new streets, a modern bridge over the River Ybbs, schools, industrial plants, a new railway station. The town was an important railway junction where large numbers of railway employees, engineers, workers and train personnel found work, among them job-seekers from Bohemia and Moravia whose native tongue was Czech. Pan-German circles protested against these immigrants, uttering shrill warnings of a systematic 'Slavization' of the town, if not of all Lower Austria. Membership of Amstetten's nationalist associations soared in the years leading up to the First World War: the German School Association, the Jahn Gymnastic Club, the Union of German Clerks, the Male Voice Choral Society. The Südmark Protection Association, which was started in Graz to promote German schools in Lower Styria, had two local branches in the little town. Nationalist fears were stoked by the example of Vienna, where there genuinely had been a large increase in the Czech population. The Federal Parliament was bogged down in venomous disputes between nationalities – between the Czechs and Germans in particular – which at times brought it to a standstill. Extreme German nationalists took these breakdowns of the multi-ethnic Viennese parliament as a reason to reject parliamentarianism in general, denouncing it as a rotten, obsolete system that had to be smashed to pieces. But as far as Amstetten was concerned, there were never any real grounds for a fear of *Überfremdung*, inundation by foreign elements; the town's German character was never remotely threatened. In the national census of 1900, only thirty-one of Amstetten's 5,670 inhabitants put Bohemian, Moravian or Slovakian as their mother tongue. It was a far cry from this handful of Czechs and Slovaks to a 'Slavization' of the town, a wave of incomers swamping its German identity.

My grandfather quickly made friends in Amstetten's pan-German circles, who welcomed the 'language-border German', as he defiantly styled himself, as a valiant ally. He had gained a wealth of first-hand experience in Tüffer and Cilli of the Germans' fight against the Slavs – a fight over language, political office, the professions, schools, pubs, shops – and he had also got to know the Czechs, who in those years protested especially vehemently against the domination of German language and culture.

When the First World War broke out, however, nationalist conflicts within the Habsburg Empire were temporarily pushed into the background. Now everyone made common cause against the Serbs, Russians, English and French. At the start of the war my grandfather was thirty-four; not that young for someone with a family trying to make a new start in an unfamiliar town, far from his friends and acquaintances and the place of his birth. His second son was born in Amstetten in September 1914. A year later he was accepted for military service, given his medical and sent to his regiment stationed in Graz.

My grandfather never talked to me about the First World War. He only told me that he was on the Isonzo Front. He said the Italians were traitors. Like the Czechs – although it was my grandmother, and perhaps also my uncle, my father's brother, rather than him who used to say that. They were all inclined to those sorts of clipped, unanswerable judgements as ways of explaining the world to me. The Americans were swine. The French were swine. The Jews – that went without saying. It was all that simple. 'The Czech swine, they strung up our poor SS by the feet in Prague,' my grandmother said accusingly when I announced later that I wanted to go to Prague. I was seventeen at the time. I don't know who the accusation was directed at: me, because I had chosen Prague of all places as my destination, or the hated Czechs. *Our poor SS*. My father was in the SS, although not in Prague. *Thank God*. I only learned much later that grandfather had been in the SS too: an honorary member.

My grandfather served on a drumhead court martial on the Southern Front from 1915 until 1916, and was then transferred to the Military Divisional Court in Graz, where he worked as a legal assistant and clerk until September 1918. His superiors commended his steady, honourable character, great industry, ready intelligence and initiative. 'Would be very well suited as an officer in the judicial service,' one wrote in a qualifications assessment in September 1917, but by then the catastrophe was upon them. The Habsburg armies were in retreat; the Empire was crumbling.

At the end of the war my grandfather was thirty-eight and embittered. He demobbed as a lieutenant and was able-bodied and unscathed – that was a blessing – but he belonged to a generation that had lost so much: not only the war and their savings but also their homeland. Grandfather still felt himself a Lower Styrian, despite the fact that he had moved away. Now his world had radically changed; it had become smaller, shabbier and poorer. Lower Styria and Carniola had been detached from Austria; Tüffer, Gottschee and Laibach suddenly lay across an international border. The whole area was Slovenian. The Slovenes, cursed as *Pervaken* and Windish agitators just days earlier, were in charge now, and it was the Germans in Slovenia who had to knuckle under.

In October 1918 the State of the Slovenes, Croats and Serbs was proclaimed in Zagreb, and a Slovenian national government was formed in Ljubljana. Amid the confusion of the end of the war and the disintegration of the Austro-Hungarian Empire, uncertainty was rife as to what would happen to the borders; no one knew what would end up in German Austria and what would be given to the new Slovenia. In Lower Styria, a Slovenian major by the name of Rudolf Maister launched a surprise raid with volunteers from the local home guard and seized control of Marburg's garrison. Military command in Graz considered mobilizing troops to recover Styria's second-largest town and surrounding area for the already reduced Austria, but the soldiers were war-weary and their discipline was suspect. Allied commissions were dispatched to establish where the border should fall.

On 27 January 1919 an American delegation visited Marburg and was received by Rudolf Maister, who had in the meantime been promoted to general. The town's German population came out onto the main square, demanding that the town should remain part of German Austria. All the German associations demonstrated: the German School Association, the Marburg Gymnastic Club, the Marburg Male Voice Choral Society with its flag. They wanted to show the world that Germans were in the

49

majority in Marburg. When the American delegation sat down for lunch in the *Narodni dom*, the Town Hall, for unexplained reasons a free-for-all broke out between demonstrators and Slovenian soldiers. The soldiers shot into the crowd; thirteen people were left dead on the square. 'Marburg's Bloody Day' took its place in the heroic chronicle of sufferings visited upon the 'language-border Germans' of Lower Styria. My grandmother talked about it as if she had been there. She could never forgive the Slovenes this atrocity, although she certainly did not know any of the victims personally. I cannot remember my grandfather ever talking about 'Marburg's Bloody Day', but perhaps I was still too little and he didn't want to scare me with gruesome stories. He preferred telling me about bloodthirsty wolves and wounded boars threatening his life in the dolines of the Hornwald.

This General Maister, who the Slovenes called a national hero and the Germans a Windish traitor, also played a certain part in our family's history. My grandfather's younger brother Ernst – identical CVs, both of them: German School Association's Elementary School in Tüffer, German Gymnasium in Cilli, German Gymnastic Club, law studies and student fraternity in Graz, pan-German politics – had returned to Lower Styria after completing his studies. He worked as a trainee for a well-known German attorney in Windischgraz (Slovenj Gradec in Slovenian) and became an active member of the Gymnastic Club, the German Choral Society and the Südmark German School Association. After the end of the Great War this keen gymnast was taken in for questioning with other fellow enthusiasts on the orders of General Maister, released, and then had a warrant issued for his arrest. The German gymnasts were allegedly planning to mount an armed insurrection against the Slovenian regime. My great-uncle, who apparently even had a price put on his head, had to flee the country. Like-minded railway workers smuggled him over the border disguised as a stoker on a goods train. He was very short-sighted and, in keeping with the fashion of the time and his status as an up-and-coming attorney, wore a pair of pince-nez at all times, even in the train driver's cab. The driver's response was often quoted in Great-Uncle Ernst's house in Amstetten with an amused smile: 'Herr Doktor, get the pince-nez off, for heaven's sake, otherwise no one'll believe you're a stoker and we'll be screwed.'

After his escape, Ernst took his law exams in Graz and then went to Amstetten, where he began working in my grandfather's, his elder brother's, practice in the autumn of 1919. Their office was on Wiener Strasse, in the same building as the City of Vienna inn; they even had a telephone, number forty-six out of seventy in Amstetten. The brothers set about becoming assimilated into the small Lower Austrian town as quickly as possible. Both my grandfather and grandmother were energetic members of the Lutheran church. No Protestant festival could pass without her baking something from her repertoire and, ever the former teacher, she attended to the churchgoers' spiritual sustenance as well by donating books to the parish lending library. In 1924 the *Protestant Parish News* of Amstetten proudly announced the library's acquisition of two new works by Pastor Ludwig Mahnert of Lower Styria: '*The Hunger Bell*, a novel from the Styrian Away from Rome Movement, and *Until You Bow Down*, a novel set during the Styrian Counter Reformation. Every member of our congregation should have read both of these books and we should all help spread word of them.' Ludwig Mahnert was a rabid German nationalist and Slovene-hater who had to flee Marburg in 1919. I remember the *Hunger Bell*, which my grandmother gave me to read when I was ten. I presume it was her who donated Mahnert's works to the lending library.

In 1925 my grandfather was elected trustee of the Protestant parish. Politically he found a home in the Greater German People's Party, which espoused a radical anti-Semitism and called for Austria's Anschluss – its union – with Germany. His younger brother threw himself into the German Gymnastic Club in Amstetten, whose activities included not just bar exercises but songs and swinging Indian clubs to musical accompaniment. The law firm above the City of Vienna inn may have been small, but it prospered; the brothers began to make a name for themselves. Their staunchly German nationalist views were no hindrance; Amstetten had its fair share of German nationalists in positions of influence, of whom some were also members of the Lutheran church. In later years the brothers' ways parted. They fell out for reasons unknown to me, but they both continued to work as attorneys in Amstetten and to live only minutes away from one another.

As a child I spent many weeks staying with my Great-Uncle Ernst in Amstetten and in his little country house on the Danube, where I was pampered by his grown-up daughter and wife, who I lovingly called Aunt Michi. I was a sort of living link between the estranged branches of the family. I stayed with my grandmother for part of the holidays and then I was sent to my great-uncle's, my third home. My first home was in Linz with my mother, my father (who really was my stepfather) and my brother and sister, who were actually my half-brother and sister, but nothing was said about that. My stepfather was an artist by profession and a passionate gardener, a passion I have inherited from him. He never made me feel that I was someone else's child, whose family lived in Amstetten and asserted an equal claim to me. When I travelled from Linz to Amstetten, I literally left my Linz family behind. The short train journey was enough to make me forget everything: our house on a hill above the town, the garden with the old fruit trees – it was as if it was all erased from my memory the moment I saw my grandmother on the platform. Then the only things that existed for me were the town of Amstetten, my grandparents and my great-uncle and aunt, who somehow shared me between them, a few weeks here, a few weeks there. I don't know what the arrangement was, but I had no objections to it. I loved them all and was loved by them all in return – showered with love, in fact. When I was staying with my great-uncle, I didn't hear or see anything of my grandmother, even though she only lived a street away. I had a gift for blanking out awkward things and people.

Great-Uncle Ernst's flat was spacious and, for the time, almost luxuriously furnished. In the bathroom there was even a bidet, whose purpose remained obscure to me for a long while. A tall, firmly locked gun cupboard stood in the passage, and I often stared longingly at its contents through the glass door. I too felt the spell cast by guns. Was it something in the blood? I cannot remember ever having touched one of my great-uncle's guns – although, when I think of hunting rifles, I smell gun oil, and by that stage there wouldn't have been any guns that needed oiling in my grandfather's house. My great-uncle's hunting days must also have been well in the past by then; deer horns and stag antlers hung on the walls as proof of earlier conquests. His son was away studying in Vienna, so I stayed in his room. The wall over the bed was covered with stuffed animals, an entire menagerie frozen in different poses: a marten on a branch ready to spring, a squirrel holding a cone in its paw, an eagle owl, a snipe, a hawk with outspread wings, a hoopoe. The dead animals stared down at me with their cold glass eyes. I suppose the toys and children's books that were always waiting for me at my great-uncle's were also his son's. I was particularly fascinated by a big war game that was kept in a sturdy box. It had plywood soldiers in German Wehrmacht uniforms, throwing hand grenades, firing rifles – some lying, some standing – or storming forwards, their rifles thrust out. There were wind-up tin tanks that threw off sparks and made rattling noises that were meant to sound like gunfire when they moved, troop carriers, cannons and even bombs, lead balls which opened up, so you could put caps in them that made a bang when they hit the ground. I don't remember any aircraft for dropping the bombs or any enemy soldiers, English or Russian, to be mowed down by the plywood soldiers. The war game was rarely brought out for me, just on special occasions.

Even as a child I was aware that my great-uncle, a colossal man with a big, gleaming bald head as round as a ball, enjoyed great respect, if not actual fear, in the family. I was correspondingly shy in his company, but he was always friendly to me. He lavished an almost idolatrous love on his dog, a small, smooth-haired cross, half fox terrier, half terrier, called Bibi. Great-Uncle Ernst always ate on his own in the dining room just with his dog, no one else – or is this my memory playing a trick on me? Is this a projection of the remoteness that he seemed to me to radiate? He spoilt Bibi with so many sponge fingers and whipped cream that over the years she grew into a yapping barrel-shaped thing, with a tiny head and spindly little legs. I remember the way my great-uncle talked, with the same intonation as my grandfather and certain words and phrases that they had both brought from Lower Styria and never given up. When he wanted to know the time, he'd ask, '*Wieviel haben wir es auf der Uhr?*' ('What do we have on the clock?')

For many years the garden at the back of his house contained a special attraction for me: a massive bomb half-embedded in the ground, amidst the ruin of what was once a summerhouse. Its bulbous, thick steel casing was battered and cracked but intact, a rusty monument to destruction that was finally cleared away one day when I wasn't there, with the remains of the structure it had shattered. The garden contained another war relic, although this one was invisible: a tortoise called Goggi, which was meant to have disappeared during an air raid and never been seen again. No one knew if Goggi had been killed by the air pressure or flying debris or if, in tortoise fashion, it had simply burrowed into the ground and never re-emerged. I remember every time I went to my great-uncle's I'd search the garden in the hope of finding this tortoise, which I only knew of from stories, or at least its shell, which I would like to have owned.

7

When I planned the trip to Prague I was seventeen. It was 1961 and the Cold War was at its peak. The trip marked the start of my estrangement from my grandmother. Prague was a breach of a taboo, a betrayal of the values in which she believed and in which I, as my father's son, should also believe. After she had failed, by invoking the memory of 'our poor SS who had been strung up by their feet in Prague', to dissuade me from my plans, she tried some cautious bribery. She suggested that, instead of going to Prague, I undertake a tour of the cities of Germany: Nuremberg, Speyer, Heidelberg, Weimar, Dresden. Gorgeous German cities, testimony to the excellence of German architecture, pearls of German culture. She said she'd gladly pay for a trip like that, broad-mindedly overlooking the fact that Weimar and Dresden were in communist East Germany. As a rule she avoided bringing up my dead father in conversations with me, but now, in her desperation, she resorted to that approach. She told me that my father had done a tour of all the German cities when he was just my age; he had even submitted a paper on one for his *Matura*: 'Cologne as an Economic Centre in the West of Germany.' That left me cold. The subject bored me and I was immediately seized by an aversion for all German cities, especially Cologne.

My father graduated from a *humanistische* Gymnasium (one with an emphasis on classical studies) in Wels, a medium-sized town in Upper Austria south of Linz, and did indeed submit a homework project on Cologne for his *Matura*, which was marked 'Good'. Otherwise, judging from his certificate, he was a rather mediocre pupil. Only in gymnastics and 'optional singing' were his achievements graded 'Very Good'.

In the autumn of 1929 he went to Graz to study law, like his father and his father's brothers before him, and like them joined a *Burschenschaft*, a student fraternity, in his first year – Germania, naturally. After winning his first duel he was *geburscht*, promoted from *Fux*, new member, to *Bursche*, full member. Germania set great store by tradition. His Graz years, as both a student and fraternity member, were as formative for him as they had been for my grandfather. Anti-Semitism was a major article of belief for the nationalist *Burschenschaften*. The Jews were to blame for everything; they had shirked the war and earned a fortune from profiteering while the national comrades had fought and suffered. Fraternity members were prohibited any contact with Jews, who were deemed unqualified to give satisfaction. Jewish fellow students were cut dead or, if the opportunity presented itself, beaten up. Graz University saw itself as a border stronghold of German science, an élite school of German nationalism and, later, of National Socialism. This was equally true of the students and teaching body.

The collapse of the Habsburg Empire had dealt Styria a critical blow. A third of its territory had been partitioned off and allotted to the Kingdom of the Serbs, Croats and Slovenes, severing significant transport links in the process. Most Austrians, rather than just German nationalists, saw a union with Germany as the only hope for their economically shattered country, which was widely written off as unviable. But the hopes invested in such a union were, if possible, even greater in Styria than elsewhere, and the indignation provoked by the conquering powers' veto of an Anschluss all the more bitter. To many Styrians, a union with Germany was also a way of keeping the, in their eyes, threatening young Yugoslav state in check. Border conflicts in the south, around places like Marburg and Radkersburg, soon spawned paramilitary groups, which also armed themselves against internal enemies – the Reds, the threat of Marxist revolution.

Graz's students played a leading role in the Styrian Heimwehr (Home Guard) groups, out of which emerged the Styrian Heimatschutz (Home Defence). Ideologically pan-German and pro-Anschluss, the Styrian Heimatschutz was the largest and most radical grouping in the Austrian Heimwehr movement. Its leader was the Judenburg attorney Walter Pfrimer: born in Marburg, studied law in Graz, member of the Ostmark (Eastern March) student fraternity, prominent in reactionary organizations such as the Südmark School Association. In 1929 clashes became increasingly frequent between the Heimatschutz and leftists, principally members of Social Democratic Republican Defence Corps, and people were wounded and killed.

In November 1929, the same month Gerhard Bast enrolled in the Legal and Political Science Faculty of Graz University, the Heimwehren organized a big march through Graz, with the Heimatschutz dashingly taking the lead. My father marched too; he had been a member of the organization for four weeks. It was considered almost a duty for Graz fraternity members to volunteer for the student battalions of the Styrian Heimatschutz, where they received basic military training.

A photo from 1930 shows my father strolling arm in arm with a friend through Graz. It is cold; they are wearing winter coats, gloves and hats and carrying walking sticks, a pair of elegant young gentlemen, carefree dandies. He enjoyed his time as a student, being away from petty bourgeois Amstetten and his strict family, outings with friends – mountaineering, climbing, skiing – fraternity life, pubs. He had his fair share of success with girls as well; he was a smart dresser, sporty, tanned, good fun. A bit of a tearaway too, sometimes. It was the Depression, but the law firm in Amstetten was doing well. On one occasion my grandfather went to Graz to check up on his son and have a serious talk. The latter met him at the train station with some friends. They hadn't left the platform before father and son started arguing, each as stubborn and quick-tempered as the other. The old man grew furious and began to curse; red in the face, the veins in their foreheads pulsing, the two of them shouted at one another, until my grandfather furiously turned on his heel and got onto the next train back, which was standing in the station. He threw the month's allowance he had brought with him on the platform, then slammed the window shut. My father went and sat with his friends in the station buffet, where they ordered beer, waved to the fuming old man and supposedly even threw empty beer glasses in his direction, although that may be a later embellishment to the story. I can't now remember who told it to me.

Alongside their carefree, cheerful selves, however, the younger generation revealed another, darker side. They had learnt to hate everything around them: the puny new state, the parliamentary democracy and the political parties, the clerics and the Bolsheviks, the capitalists and the Jews, the foreign powers who vetoed the Anschluss with Germany, and the Slovenes 'who stole Lower Styria from us'. They wanted to subvert society, turn it upside down, smash all the institutions of state; everything should be subordinated to a strong leader. 'Unquestioning obedience in the service of the German Volk; belief in the identity of the Volk; unity and purity of the Volk.' They were prepared to uphold these principles fanatically (a term of approbation to them) and uncompromisingly, to fight political opponents, dissenters, Christian Socialists and Reds without quarter, regardless of casualties or state laws.

In 1930 my father visited Kočevje across the border in Yugoslavia; perhaps he went hunting with my grandfather; he was a passionate hunter himself. There's a photo of him with a friend, who might be the same one with whom he strolled through Graz; the picture is too small to tell. They are standing arm-in-arm in a garden, a high brick wall behind them, both dressed for a ball in dark suits with white dress handkerchiefs, one in an ordinary tie and the other a bow tie. They are smiling confidently, light-hearted young fellows, small town beaus; they look like they are just about to ask a couple of pretty girls to dance.

On 12 September 1931 Walter Pfrimer launched a regional putsch with armed units of the Styrian Heimatschutz. They blockaded major traffic routes in Upper Styria and occupied towns; the Judenburg attorney, a huge, shaven-headed man, proclaimed himself the new head of state. His putsch received hardly any popular support, however; the other Heimwehr organizations failed to mobilize, and the Austrian army was able to suppress it almost without a fight. Pfrimer fled abroad, to Yugoslavia – to Maribor, of all places, the town where he was born. I don't think my father was involved in the putsch; he was not arrested at any rate nor even reported to the authorities. But he was probably already toying with the idea of switching from the Heimatschutz to the Nazis. Ideologically the two groups did not differ fundamentally from one another: both were German nationalist, radically anti-democratic and anti-Semitic. In 1931 the NSDAP (Hitler Movement) – the qualifier was necessary to differentiate it from other, antagonistic National Socialist splinter groups – had begun to step up its propaganda in Styria. It had scored a huge success in the German elections in September 1930, winning 6 million votes, which played well in Austria. The Nazis canvassed students particularly intensively, with meetings, posters, flyers and turgid rhetoric in *Der Kampf*, the Styrian National Socialists' paper published in Graz:

> The brown-shirted student is implacably resolved to crush all opposition and to place his entire labour wholly at the service of a new, German Germany.

Once again incorporated into the entirety of the Volk, the National Socialist student sees with inner belief his impending mission to be a standard bearer of an idea of the future, a Führer in a time of struggle, whose goals have undergone a reassessment with their evolution into the essence of National Socialism.

The failed putsch gave the National Socialists a welcome opportunity to canvass frustrated Heimatschutz members. 'Come to Adolf Hitler! Become National Socialists!' exhorted *Der Kampf* with them in mind.

On 30 October 1931 my father accepted this call and joined the NSDAP in Graz; he was given Membership Number 612.972. He wouldn't have worried about his family reproaching him for this step. My grandfather had already joined the Nazi party in August of the same year and been assigned Membership Number 514.334.

When I wonder about my grandfather's influence on my father, I often think of the Kaltenbrunner family, which displays certain similarities with my family on my father's side. Hugo Kaltenbrunner, the father of Ernst Kaltenbrunner, who became the Head of the Reich Security Main Office (RSHA) and was hanged at Nuremberg in 1946, was born in a small town in Upper Austria in 1875; my grandfather in 1880. Both studied law in Graz, joined fraternities – Arminia and Germania, respectively – and became attorneys. The sons emulated the fathers: law studies in Graz, student fraternities, Heimwehr, NSDAP, SS. One important difference: Hugo Kaltenbrunner did not enthusiastically join the National Socialists early on, like my grandfather, but kept a certain distance. The Kaltenbrunner family, incidentally, came from Linz and knew my mother and stepfather, although they were not friends. In May 1931, in Linz, Hildegard Gfrerer, my mother, had married the bank official and artist Hans Pollack, whose name I bear.

My natural father was not yet twenty-one when he joined the party; my grandfather was already fifty-one. After the First World War (like Hugo Kaltenbrunner) he had voted for the Greater German People's Party, which had resulted from the merging of a number of German nationalist, anti-Semitic parties. So what now made the prosperous Amstetten attorney Rudolf Bast abandon his safe middle-class ways and join the Nazis, who were a pack of vicious bully boys, although increasingly influential?

I don't know. I never asked my grandfather; I was too young. He died in 1960 and – a result of his alcoholism – barely communicated with anyone towards the end of his life. I never asked my grandmother either. I didn't ask anyone at all about their pre-war lives then, not because I didn't dare but because there was something like a silent understanding between us not to ask any personal questions.

When my grandfather was arrested after the war, he gave an outrageous explanation for his early entry into the NSDAP and correspondingly low Membership Number. He said that in fact he had only joined the party in April 1938, after the Anschluss. The day after joining, he had been celebrating his name day in the tap room in Amstetten when the then leader of Amstetten's NSDAP branch, Wolf Mitterdorfer, had come over to collect his quarterly dues, 3.90 schillings. My grandfather said that when he produced a ten-schilling note, Mitterdorfer had explained that, for those dues, his membership could be backdated to make it look as if he had been a member of the party when it was illegal. So then my grandfather, in an expansive mood because he had been drinking, gave him 100 schillings. If you work out the time those dues would cover, you arrive at August 1931 as the date he joined the Nazis. So in fact the early party membership was just an invention; he had never been active in the banned party, he was never a fanatic of the outlawed party. It was all just the alcohol talking, a drunken fantasy.

The student Gerhard Bast joined the 38th Regiment of the SS in Graz and was assigned SS Number 23064 on 18 January 1932. That at least is the date given in an index entry in his SS file, but in a CV also in his files he wrote that he joined the Party and the SS at the same time in October 1931. It is quite possible he did; bureaucratic precision was not one of the National Socialists' strengths at that stage – that came later. Heinrich Himmler conceived of the SS as the racial and political élite of the state of the future, the new aristocracy – a sworn community of men of pure Aryan blood distinguished by pseudo-Teutonic rituals and insignia and black uniforms with the death's head on the cap and the runic double 'S' on the collar patch, they were to be a dark knightly order of *Übermenschen*. At this point the only organizations of the SS in Styria were in the university towns of Graz and Leoben. Students, blue-collar workers, minor office workers; the numbers were modest, many were unemployed and few could afford a proper uniform. In Graz the thirty or so members of the SS met at the Red Tower Inn, presided over by the so-called 'Nazi landlady'. Unlike the Austrian NSDAP, which had its own leadership, the Austrian SS reported directly to the Reichsführer of the SS, Heinrich Himmler. Graz's Nazis generally met in the Steinfelder Beer Hall; they felt as at home among beer fumes as the student fraternities. They were very active, organizing talks and discussions – 'Secure your seats! No entry to Jews!' – film screenings, collections for needy party members, hiking tours, skiing schools and summer-solstice celebrations. The SS were used as security for the party's meetings and to disrupt those of their opponents. They fought running battles, particularly with supporters of the Republican Defence Corps.

In July 1932 Graz Regional Court fined my father ten schillings for the offence of intentional bodily harm and affray, under Criminal Law §411. Ten days later he was issued with a firearms licence for a hunting rifle and what was known as a parlour rifle. As a precaution he had applied for the licence in his native Amstetten, rather than in Styria. In January 1933 the licence was extended to include a pistol under 18 centimetres in length.

In 1932, in addition to his SS activities, he took on the job of Fencing Guardian in the Germania fraternity, like his father thirty years before him. He fought duels, went mountain climbing, undertook lengthy skiing tours, travelled to Gottschee to hunt and took the State History of Law exam with passable success. It seems remarkable that he did any studying at all.

Graz was troubled ground in those years. The confrontations between the National Socialists on the one hand and the Social Democrats or Communists on the other were becoming increasingly brutal, with both sides seeking to exploit the clashes for their own ends. In September 1932 an eighteen-year-old student, SS man and student fraternity member died in a brawl in Graz. 'Red Murder Claims Victim in Graz. SS Man August Assmann Stabbed to Death by Marxists,' ran *Der Kampf*'s headline. His funeral was turned into a massive propaganda rally. At the head of the procession marched the SS, the Hitler Youth, the SA band and a colour party with swastika flags; then came the wreath-bearers, with pride of place given to a big wreath of roses and forget-me-nots sent by Adolf Hitler, then the hearse, flanked by SS men with torches and student fraternity members in full uniform, and finally delegations from the German Gymnasts, the pan-German Schönerer Association, the Front Fighters' Association and the Heimatschutz. *Der Kampf* reported a funeral procession of many thousands:

> By the time the procession reached the graveyard, night had already fallen. The moon's wan light recalled that cast on the ghostly funeral procession marking young Siegfried's death and the torches of the SS men flickered darkly.

The National Socialists were aficionados of bombastic pathos and histrionic staging. This was a preliminary demonstration of strength and power, a foretaste of the fanaticized masses that a few years later would lead Hitler to confer on Graz the title 'City of the People's Insurrection'. A favourite stunt of the National Socialists was to let off paper mortars, cardboard containers filled with black gunpowder, fitted with a fuse and either thrown or planted in public places. It was a small step from these to lethal bomb attacks. When the Bavarian Minister of Justice, Dr Hans Frank,* visited Graz in May 1933, four months after Hitler seized power in Germany, the police and army were drafted in to prevent any demonstrations of solidarity. The Nazis went on the rampage: they threw dozens of paper mortars and, in front of the Red Tower Inn, the meeting point of the Graz SS, released a live pig with the names of Dollfuss, the Austrian Chancellor, and Vaugoin, the Minister of Defence, painted in red on its back.

Dollfuss was moving towards an increasingly authoritarian regime. In September 1933 he abolished parliament and established a corporate state, based on conservative Roman Catholic and Italian fascist principles. Henceforth, rule was to be by decree and his party, the Fatherland Front, was to replace all others. Steps had already been taken against the opposition, however. In June 1933 the National Socialist terror reached its peak. Near Krems on the Danube, SA men threw hand grenades into a column of police auxiliaries, killing one and wounding many others. The Dollfuss administration responded by banning the NSDAP in Austria, and dissolved the Styrian Heimatschutz at the same time. Leading National Socialists were arrested across the country, but plenty still managed to escape to Germany where they joined the nascent 'Austrian Legion' in Bavaria.

*Hans Michael Frank (1900–46), legal adviser to Adolf Hitler and NSDAP, and Governor-General of Poland, who sent hundreds of thousands of Jews and Poles to their deaths. He was hanged at Nuremberg on 1 October 1946.

That summer my father went to Laško, to visit Aunt Pauline and his Slovenian Uncle Drolc, the church organist and choir-master. The student from Graz had shaved his head to show off the duelling scars that ran across his skull like white furrows. He was twenty-two but looked older. They hiked over the hills of the Tüffer range, through beech and chestnut woods, past little farms where the owners served their own wine, up to the ruined castle from where they could look over the whole Sann valley, and on their return drank beer in the Horiak or, as it had long been called by then, Henke Hotel. It was a hot, rainless summer, the air hung in the narrow, dusty lanes of the quiet little town, and the country folk said that there would be a good vintage that year and a fine chestnut crop.

8

My grandparents' home in Preinsbacher Strasse in Amstetten was a two-storey 1870s building with a turret on the roof where doves nested. I remember the cool semi-darkness of the stairwell and the stylized, cast-iron lion's head with gaping jaws which crowned the baluster at the foot of the stairs. Sometimes I stuck my finger in its maw as a cheap test of courage, and I always felt relieved when it didn't bite me. My grandfather's office was on the half landing, my grandparents' flat on the first floor, and on the floor above lived a man who my grandmother scornfully called the 'Communist', as if that was all one could say about such a person, and even that was probably too much. The municipal housing office had allocated him a flat in the building after my grandparents, its owners, had fled the Russians in 1945 and, after they came back, they never had any grounds to give him notice: his behaviour was faultless and he always paid the rent.

Next to the building ran a little stream, which had been confined to a deep, walled channel some time before I was born and only burst its banks at high water, when it would flood the street and the cellar. Squeezed between this and the house was a tiny strip of garden, not a metre wide, where my grandfather grew flowers: fire lilies, dahlias, snapdragons and roses. 'My Riviera,' he would call their gorgeous, lush blooms. Somehow he seemed lost, that powerfully built man with the bristly little goatee standing there among his flowers, in a bed so narrow that he could hardly turn around, always dressed as if he was about to go hunting at any moment: Styrian hat, Loden jacket, knickerbockers, thick wool stockings, sturdy walking shoes. In the autumn and winter he wore a grey-speckled overcoat over the jacket, a so-called Schladminger, and he always kept a penknife in a holder of soft, grey buckskin in a little pocket in his knickerbockers. I cannot remember ever having seen him in long trousers.

Further along Preinsbacher Strasse stood the Regional Court and prison, whose barred windows looked onto my grandparents' house across a weed-infested field that was the preserve of the local dogs. After 1945, Soviet administrative headquarters took over the building. Two monumental portraits of Lenin and Stalin framed with electric light bulbs hung either side of the entrance and, above them, a large, five-pronged red star. Under the ill-assorted pair of brothers, like the cartoon book characters Max, with a bald head, and Moritz, with a walrus moustache, Russian soldiers stood guard. They wore tightly belted, dirty-green greatcoats with tails that flared out like ballerinas' tutus, and their iron-tipped boots clattered on the cobbles when they marched. The guards at the gate had sub-machine guns with round drum magazines slung over their backs and forage caps with the red star on their heads. My grandfather got on well with the Russians. He spoke in Slovenian, they in Russian: *dobar dan, sdraswujte, živio*. He had returned to Amstetten in the autumn of 1950, by which time the Russian occupation had lost much of its terror for former National Socialists.

My grandmother used to tell me that the people in prison had all been arrested by the Russians, and then add that they were innocent. According to her they were sent to camps in the frozen wastelands of Siberia not because they'd done anything wrong but simply because they had been denounced by the Communists, the Reds. She said that it was just like when the Nazis, 'our people', as she called them, had been put in prison during the so-called *Systemzeit*,* the Weimar Republic, although

*'The days of the system', often abbreviated to 'the system', this Nazi term of indictment referred specifically to Weimar's parliamentary system of government and generally to everything they hated about the period 1918–33.

it wasn't the communists who had denounced them then (they were proscribed too) but Dollfuss's people, the Blacks. It wasn't easy for a child to find his way around in this world. I sometimes tried to imagine what the Blacks or the Reds looked like, but I found it hard, because I didn't know any. I only knew what the Nazis looked like.

After the NSDAP was banned in 1933, a number of prominent Amstetten Nazis were imprisoned in Preinsbacher Strasse. My grandfather was not arrested initially, although the authorities had their eye on him: his politics were common enough knowledge in the small town. In July 1933 he was reported for allegedly calling out 'Heil Hitler' to some detainees as he was walking past the prison. The police investigated the incident and established that inmates had indeed been singing the Horst Wessel song and other banned Nazi songs at the tops of their voices and greeting passers-by, including the attorney Dr Rudolf Bast, with 'Heil Hitler', but that the latter had responded at most with 'Heil'. 'Dr Bast definitely did not call out Heil Hitler.'

The ban on political participation and the dissolution of the party and its subordinate organizations kept the Nazis in check for a while, but they soon resumed their activities. They wanted to show that they weren't going to be intimidated by the state. They graffitied walls with swastikas and rebellious slogans like 'Trotz Verbot nicht tot!' ('We are outlaws but we are not dead!'), wore white stockings as markers of their affiliation and, instead of the banned swastika, white slips of paper in their lapels or the emblem of the German Gymnastic League, four big Fs – Frisch, Fromm, Fröhlich, Frei (Fresh, God-Fearing, Happy, Free) – which were arranged in such a way that they look remarkably like a swastika. The authorities responded with fines and prison sentences, making it a criminal offence to sport the substitute insignia, sing the Horst Wessel song or, obviously, call out 'Heil

Hitler' or '*Pfui* Dollfuss' ('To Hell with Dollfuss'). There were also songs by local composers and poets the Nazis took up. Especially popular in Amstetten, which is not far from the Wachau region, was a song about the 'German Wachau', which was sung in the streets and in pubs – there was even a record – until it was banned for its National Socialist sympathies. The lyrics are exemplary of the nationalist pathos prized by the Nazis.

> Awake, German Wachau!
>
> Why does the Danube race with such alarm
> Through the broad, German land?
> From castle to castle echoes the refrain
> When will the Ostmark rise again?
> Say, is our brother homeward bound
> Home at last to the Fatherland?
> . . .
> But all around, paid in foreign gold,
> Hordes of enemies wait
> To enslave us with insolent flood
> Then o'er it boils, the German blood!
> Lo, the whole Volk shall repay
> Who'er so bold would it betray!
>
> Awake, German Wachau!
> *Heil* Nibelungengau!
>
> Once more the brilliant light of dawn
> Shall rise from darkest night
> And on one race of brothers shine
> From the Danube to the Rhine
> O'er every castle I see banners wave
> And our heroes rising from the grave.

The Nazi prisoners often bawled so loudly that they could be heard in the well-to-do houses behind the prison in Villensstrasse, whose owners sometimes complained. In general they were said to lead a high old life. One scandalized burgher reported that they had schnitzel and wine delivered to their cells by the Todt and Sengstbratl inns, and fresh rolls and ice cream by the Julius Exel Steam Bakery and Confectioners.

In January 1934 the attacks grew more frequent in Amstetten. Night after night unknown individuals let off paper mortars in the main square, outside the municipal buildings, in front of the residences of prominent supporters of the corporate state, wherever they could get away with it. Although the primitive explosive devices didn't cause much damage, the message was hard to ignore: We are back; we are to be reckoned with. Unable to discover the culprits, the authorities arrested a group of prominent National Socialists, including the pharmacist Wolf Mitterdorfer and the attorney Dr Rudolf Bast: 'both well-known leaders of the swastika-wearers', according to a Social Democrat newspaper. Wolf Mitterdorfer had founded the local branch of the Anti-Semitic League with others of like mind in 1919; later he was the National Socialist representative on Amstetten municipal council until the party was banned in 1933. Mitterdorfer was also an active member of the small Protestant community that acted as a reservoir for German nationalists.

When the arrested Nazis were taken to the station to be transferred to Kaisersteinbruch detention camp at Bruck an der Leitha, hundreds of their comrades assembled and, screaming slogans of defiance, formed an escort for the detainees; some even lay on the tracks to stop the train leaving. It took a contingent of police and soldiers to break up the demonstrators and restore peace.

In the detention camps of the authoritarian corporate state, the largest of which was in Wöllersdorf in Lower Austria, Dollfuss's political opponents were interned: Communists and National

Socialists to begin with and, after the fighting in February 1934,[*] Social Democrats as well. Many of the detainees were sent to the camps pre-emptively, for harbouring 'party political attitudes that are known to the authorities' or on suspicion of preparing subversive acts, without this having to be proved. Known National Socialists could also be summonsed to pay for damages caused by explosions or graffiti, even if they had nothing to do with the incidents. Often arbitrarily interpreted, the Nazis exploited these laws in their propaganda to portray themselves as victims, martyrs for the nationalist cause languishing in Kaisersteinbruch, 'Dollfuss's hell.' Nazis arrested in Amstetten were normally sent to Kaisersteinbruch. After the Anschluss Wolf Mitterdorfer, now Mayor of Amstetten, took pride in the fact that, relative to its population, more 'illegals' from Amstetten had been interned in Kaisersteinbruch than from any other Austrian city. It was hardly a coincidence: at the last free elections in 1932 the National Socialists in Amstetten won over a quarter of the votes.

From Kaisersteinbruch, my grandfather was transferred to Wöllersdorf, where he was detained until June 1934. Then, according to a NSDAP questionnaire that he filled out in May 1938, he went to Yugoslavia, where he stayed until March 1935. This is puzzling. He wrote, '*Konfinierung* to Yugoslavia until 1.3.1935,' but a *Konfinierung* is a judicial limitation of residence to a particular place. It is hard to understand how my grandfather, who had had Austrian nationality since 1921, could have been assigned a compulsory place of residence in Yugoslavia. Or is the story of the *Konfinierung* an invention to burnish the legend of his martyrdom? I tend to think that he went to Yugoslavia of his own accord to escape the supervision of Dollfuss's police. I have not been able to find out whether he stayed with his relatives in

[*]An armed uprising of Austrian workers on 12 February 1934 was crushed after four days of fighting by Dollfuss's government troops and elements of the Heimwehr, and the Social Democratic Party was banned.

Tüffer, or in Gottschee, where he had close friends, but in any event he was not the only Nazi in Yugoslavia at the time. After the unsuccessful putsch of July 1934, a string of party members from Styria and Carinthia retreated across the border. My grandfather also certainly met Ernst Kaltenbrunner, who was arrested like him in the middle of January, in Kaisersteinbruch. The tall Linz lawyer with the scarred, horsey face was the most prominent of the five hundred or so Nazis in Kaisersteinbruch and he organized the hunger strike, which led to the camp's closure in April 1934.

My grandfather was repeatedly bound over to pay compensation for damages. The authorities can't have envisaged any difficulties collecting money from an attorney with a thriving practice, but he flatly refused to pay anything, citing his lack of means. He had already signed over the house with the turret on Preinsbacher Strasse to my grandmother.

9

The Julius Exel Steam Bakery and Confectioners on Amstetten's main square, which was alleged to have delivered fresh rolls and ice cream to the Nazis in prison in 1934, is testimony to the constancy of small-town life. It has outlasted the Christian corporate state, the Third Reich and the post-war period; its creations are timeless. As a child, the confectioner's was a fixed point for me as well in Amstetten. I'd be taken there by my grandmother and each time I would have to perform a lovely, low bow to old Frau Exel, which earned me a portion of ice cream with whipped cream and wafers. '*Der Exel*' – as my grandmother always called the confectioner's, referring to the husband, although I only ever set eyes on the old woman – was the first stop on a tour of Amstetten's business community that my grandmother and I used to take at the end of the 1940s and the start of the 1950s. Holding her hand, I would be led from one establishment to the next, from Exel's to the Good Shepherd Chemist, run by a brother of the former mayor Wolf Mitterdorfer, and other shops, whose names have slipped my mind, everywhere to be introduced to grandmother's acquaintances and friends – all former Nazis, as I later found out – with the phrase: 'This is Gerhard's son.'

These words always called forth an enthusiasm that even a child of elementary-school age could tell was affected. People stroked my hair, pinched my cheeks; some women even tried to kiss me, which I found disgusting, and exclaimed how I had grown, how like my father I looked and so on, and then tears would well in the women's eyes, my grandmother's included. I patiently submitted to all this, since I knew I could generally expect a substantial reward when the unwanted endearments ceased – I was a greedy child and easily corruptible. Then they'd begin to talk over my head in low tones about Gerhard: how dashing, honourable and decent he had been and how cruelly fate had treated him. This didn't interest me very much, since there was nothing I associated with the name Gerhard. I don't think I ever saw a picture of my father at that time. And no one explained to me why I had one father in Linz who was alive, married to my mother and treated me like his own son, and another in Amstetten, who was evidently dead. Until I was twelve or thirteen, no one thought it advisable to explain these complicated family relations to me. I didn't rack my brains over their mysterious configuration, either; I accepted them as they were, and that was that. Of course, at some point I knew how things stood: that my rightful father was dead, that he had been called Gerhard Bast and that he came from Amstetten, where my beloved grandparents lived, who I had all to myself. My two older siblings in Linz had no claim on them at all. I think I was fourteen when my mother, choosing her words cautiously, intimated what my father had done in the war: SS, Gestapo. That was quite a shock in itself, but I soon got over it. She didn't go into any details.

'If anyone asks you what your father did, say he was a government counsellor,' my grandmother instructed me. I didn't learn much more than this from her. But that wasn't just her fault. I could have asked her and I failed to do so.

With us, no one asked any questions. That was the problem.

When my grandmother paraded me through Amstetten to be admired and petted like some Little Lord Fauntleroy, it was annoying but, at the same time, I enjoyed the attention of the grown-ups and the helpings of ice cream and whipped cream that invariably came my way, and the final treat: the marzipan potatoes. Produced at a confectioner's called Garn's – rather than Exel's – which I visited incognito, so to speak, without being proudly shown off to anyone, these delicacies always marked the apogee of our progress through the small town. The Amstetten marzipan potatoes – balls rolled in cocoa powder with a layer of marzipan on the outside, scored to make them look like real sauté potatoes, a layer of biscuit and a rich, dark cream in the middle – are something I still think of nostalgically today. My grandmother, who spoiled me thoroughly, went so far as to send her beloved grandson marzipan potatoes at his boarding school.

For herself, she was tremendously thrifty. If we went to a restaurant, which was seldom, she would order a schnitzel for me and a plain broth for herself, nothing else. She was modest, but not easily satisfied. I remember how embarrassing I found the way she would always send her soup back, because it was too cold or too salty or in some other way unpalatable. 'This is simply inedible,' she'd say severely, and the waiter would take the bowl away unquestioningly.

10

On 25 July 1934 units of the Austrian SS staged an attempted coup, in the course of which the Austrian Chancellor Engelbert Dollfuss was murdered. The Graz student Gerhard Bast is supposed to have reacted to the news of the death of the diminutive Chancellor with the contemptuous remark, 'Dollfuss has gone broke,' which earned him three months' detention without trial. Whether the authorities knew of his membership of the proscribed SS is doubtful. Fortunately for him he had already completed his law degree a few months before and acquired the Absolutorium, the leaving certificate allowing him to work as a lawyer, which attested that his academic performance 'had met all the requirements defined by university regulations'.

When it came to academic performance, the Graz university authorities were not especially demanding. In the 1930s the university was a hotbed of National Socialist activity. In June 1933, shortly before the party was banned, Nazi students took over the main university building for several hours, hoisting a large swastika flag on the roof, barricading the entrances with benches and only allowing in teachers they knew to be sympathizers, which was a considerable number. After the ban on the party individual professors and assistants were dismissed because of their National Socialist views, but the Nazis remained the dominant force among the students. They brought out an illegal combat paper named *Aufbruch* ('Uprising'), graffitied slogans, threw mortars, got into fights with political opponents and went up into the mountains to light swastika-shaped fires that could be seen for miles or mark out giant swastikas in the snow with their skis. There were plenty of ways to publicize the banned party.

At Easter in 1934 my father went with some friends on a skiing tour of the Grosse Bösenstein in the Rottenmanner Tauern. He took a photograph of three young men and a girl sitting on a group of rocks in the snow: nice, cleancut-looking youngsters in puffed-out skiing trousers and knickerbockers, their shirtsleeves rolled up, their stockings rolled down, with a big snowfield behind them. One can't tell from the picture whether they have trodden out a swastika with their hickory skis. I don't know who his companions are: fellow students perhaps, or friends from Amstetten or the party or the SS; presumably the girl was a girl-friend of one of them.

The Nazis attached great importance to sport, especially as a form of physical training for young people: Hitler wanted young Germans to be 'tough as leather, swift as greyhounds, hard as Krupp steel', although he didn't in any way measure up to this ideal himself. The outlawed SS frequently went up into the mountains together; the isolation was perfectly suited to cland-destine meetings and activities to bolster *esprit de corps*, solstice fires and the so-called Yule trips, tours taken at Christmas by like-minded pagans. In his Teutonic mania Heinrich Himmler wanted to replace the Christian Christmas, at least within the SS, with the Yuletide festival, which the Teutonic peoples had celebrated on the winter solstice. December was accordingly to be renamed Yule, and the indispensable Christmas tree the Yule Fir.

My father was a fervent mountain climber and skier; he used every free weekend to go into the mountains, often with Nazi party members. Under 31 January 1937 his journal reads: 'Forsteralm. SS downhill race, heavy wet snow, crumbly snow, good weather.' On 13 March he climbed with skis from Liezen over the Hochtor to the Liezen hut; the next day he laid first tracks over the Kleinmölbing and Hochmölbing to the Kreuz-spitze. On his way down he had an encounter that seemed worth

78

mentioning in his journal: 'Met Dr Kaltenbrunner.' By this stage Dr Ernst Kaltenbrunner was head of the entire Austrian SS; one can't tell from the note whether the meeting was planned or coincidental.

On 10 December 1935 my father was awarded his degree of Doctor Juris in Graz. He had started working as a law clerk in Amstetten Regional Court shortly before, as part of his practical training to become an attorney. On receiving his doctorate he was assigned to St Pölten District Court, but he only worked there for a few weeks before he was barred on suspicion of National Socialist activity. He lodged an appeal against his suspension, which was unsuccessful. The Higher Regional Court Executive in Vienna judged that recalling him would be extremely detrimental to the reputation of justice in the eyes of the patriotic population who knew of his anti-government activity. He lodged another appeal. The charges levelled against him, originating in 'Fatherland circles in his place of residence' – Amstetten – were entirely unfounded. The imputation that he was working for a prohibited party was malicious slander, he wrote, before turning to his father's political views:

My father Dr Rudolf Bast, an attorney in Amstetten, is and always has been a nationalist. As such he has fought for *Deutschtum* on the language border since childhood and made constant sacrifices for its sake. He has not just discovered his *Deutschtum* two years ago. As a language-border German, he has also had the character not to change his outlook but to uphold it constantly and in all circumstances. He has held these nationalist views since he was a child and so long before the NSDAP ever entered the political arena. He cannot therefore be stigmatized with membership of a banned party on the basis of these nationalist views. Nor did so-called 'Fatherland circles' used to have any quarrel with them. But now 'another wind' is blowing and men of dubious honour have the chance to get their own back on my father and his family. Not because of his nationalist views, which one would well understand any language-border German holding even today, but purely and simply because my father and his family are Protestants and my father happens also to be a trustee of the Amstetten Protestant parish.

Barred from working in court, my father joined his father's law firm in Amstetten as a trainee and continued to be active in the outlawed SS, where the most radical elements congregated. In the summer of 1936 he became head of the 3rd (Amstetten) Battalion of the 3rd Regiment, which was later renamed the 52nd Regiment. The SS men – students, workers, teachers, commercial employees – had the primitive basics of racial conflict drummed into them. They were instructed to spy on the authorities and their political opponents; 'to make a note of those Reich German cars which fail to display a swastika pennant when driving through Austria and to identify any German citizens who speak in a derogatory fashion about the National Socialist regime'. Informers' reports were passed on to the Gestapo in Germany.

Under mounting pressure from the German Reich, in July 1936 Chancellor Kurt Schuschnigg signed an agreement with Hitler in which he declared himself ready to harmonize Austrian foreign policy with German interests, while Hitler in return promised to respect Austria's sovereignty and put a curb on the outlawed Austrian National Socialists. As in Germany, the takeover of power in Austria was to proceed as far as possible under a cloak of legality. After the July Agreement, Nazi Germany stepped up its official propaganda in Austria, while the Austrian government attempted to deny the banned Austrian Nazis any public profile – a paradox that undermined the authority of the corporate state's institutions.

In October 1936 a detachment of the German National Socialist Motor Corps (NSKK) led by Adolf Hühnlein – twenty-five cars adorned with swastika pennants – conducted a 'Visiting Tour' of a host of Austrian towns, prompting demonstrations and clashes between Austrian Nazis and the authorities. When the cavalcade rolled into Amstetten, it was greeted by ranks of cheering Nazis. My grandfather stood in the front row, calling out '*Heil* Hitler!' to the drivers. Reprimanded by a policeman, he shouted to Hühnlein, 'Greetings officially forbidden. *Heil!*'

For this the fifty-six-year-old attorney Rudolf Bast was sentenced to forty-two days' detention. I presume he served his sentence in Amstetten prison, with a view onto his house in Preinsbacher Strasse. He even mentioned the incident two years later in the NSDAP personal questionnaire: '6 weeks detention for greeting Korpsführer Hühnlein on 4.10.1936.'

Just under a week after he had protested his innocence, at length, in his appeal to the Federal Supreme Court in Vienna, my father was arrested with seven others on a charge of illegal membership of the SS. This was in April 1937. Dr Gerhard Bast was accused of being head of the 3rd (Amstetten) Battalion of the 3rd Regiment stationed in Krems and of having transmitted a range of orders to subordinates in this capacity, including Himmler's Marriage and Engagement Order, under which members of the SS could only marry women who, like themselves, had undergone strict racial testing. He had, in addition, collected membership dues and attended secret SS meetings. The authorities had only uncovered the fringes of the subversive network, however. In the CV he later produced for the Secret State Police office, my father wrote of the period when the Nazis were outlawed: 'I served throughout prohibition. In Graz I was a troop leader and deputy of the battalion. From May 1936 I commanded the Amstetten Battalion. And, after the arrest of the Regimental Commander of 52nd Regiment, I

81

commanded that too until my arrest. In the meantime I also worked for the intelligence service of the SS.'

What did his work for the intelligence service of the outlawed SS consist of? Was it limited to taking down the licence plates of German motor vehicles that drove through Austria without swastika pennants and spying on Reich Germans who disparaged the National Socialist regime, or was there more to it than that? In any event, its activities were not discussed at the trial in St Pölten. Like the other accused he only confessed to the bare minimum, to what the authorities knew already. If arrested, the SS instructed its members to deny everything that could not be proved against them in black and white. '*Sagst du ja, bleibst du da, sagst du nein, gehst du heim*' ('Confess, you stay under arrest. Deny, you're home and dry').

In this case, my father did not go home immediately but was sentenced to six months' detention by the State Security Commissar for the City of St Pölten and to a further four months' close arrest by St Pölten District Court. This last judgement was quashed by the Supreme Court on the grounds of being too lenient. His fellow defendants were convicted too: a teacher, an electrical engineer, a bookkeeper, a labourer and three commercial clerks. At twenty-six, the trainee attorney Dr Gerhard Bast was the youngest of the group.

In December 1937 he was granted a three-month reprieve; two months later there was a general amnesty for all political offences.

11

The first thing my father did on his release was go on a long holiday. At the end of January 1938 he drove to the favourite skiing spot of Amstettners, the Rottenmanner Tauern, where he may also have hoped to escape the surveillance of the authorities who kept a keen eye on National Socialists, despite the July Agreement between Schuschnigg and Hitler.

In February one of the SS men who had been convicted with him at St Pölten a few months before, and then amnestied, was arrested in Pöchlarn. A teacher by profession, he had been caught at a meeting with fellow subversives with incriminating material in his briefcase, including a letter to a contact in which he gave a description of himself: 'For ease of recognition: I am wearing a black battledress jacket with white lapels, white cap, brown trousers, and white socks. In short, I look like Göhring [*sic*].' The outlawed Nazis no longer took great pains to conceal themselves. Initially the authorities suspected Dr Bast of also being involved in the affair, but enquiries established that he was skiing.

He stayed with friends in the 1,600-metre-high Planner hut, from where they went on long skiing tours: Kleiner Rotbühel, Grosser Rotbühel, Jochspitze, Schreinl, Schoberspitze, Bärneck and Gstemmerzinken. Every day a different route, climbing with skins on their skis, skiing down in powder snow, corn snow, crumbly snow, spending evenings in the mountain hut. A couple of women came along too, one of whom was Trude Lipp-Terler, who became Women's Guardian of the German Reich's Physical Education League in Styria after the Anschluss. According to his journal, my father spent three weeks in the Planner hut, amazingly long for a skiing holiday, but the weather was ideal: sunny days, cold nights, lots of snow. 'Gstemmer with Trude Lipp-Terler and Gerti Elger. Down to Neualm in magnificent snow with Ernstl and Balo. Neualm with Trude Trogger, Gerti and Trude L.-T. Good snow. Very jolly and merry.' A photo shows him sitting between two women in the snow; all three are tanned and laughing, care-free, nice young people enjoying life. 'Between two haystacks...' he has jokingly, but not very gallantly, written on the back.

I wonder whether it is conceivable that a militant National Socialist and member of the outlawed SS had nothing better to do so close to the Anschluss, which was clearly in the air, than bury himself away far from political events in a remote ski hut with friends, climb snow-covered peaks, lay tracks on deep, virgin slopes and spend his evenings in the hut with Trude and Gerti, between whom he couldn't decide, like Buridan's Ass. Perhaps this was all a clever front, and the journal entries were only meant for the prying eyes of the police and examining magistrates. Perhaps they held secret meetings in the Planner hut, the Stall-Alm, the Lüarchkaralm, at which arrangements were made for the coup.

In Styria the National Socialists were pressing for action. They didn't want to wait any longer and were doing everything they could to goad the corporate state, already weakened and destabi-lized by Adolf Hitler's aggressive stance, into mobilizing its armed forces against them, kill one of their number and thus provoke a military intervention by Germany. On the evening of 19 February, large rallies took place in Graz and other towns in Styria. The Nazis wore swastika armbands, shouted '*Heil* Hitler' and slogans like 'One People, One Reich, One Führer' and sang banned songs. Pictures of Hitler were sold openly and met with a ready market. In Graz Hitler's supporters marched through the streets with torches and flags; a young man climbed onto the Town Hall and to ringing applause ran up a swastika flag that was immediately taken down by the police. But the authorities were no longer able to break up the demonstrators.

The rallies continued for days. In Graz the National Socialists had seized the initiative; swastikas flew over the streets. Schuschnigg's Fatherland Front tried to show its strength with patriotic demonstrations: '*Bis zum Tod: Rot-Weiss-Rot! Österreich!*' ('To the death: Red White Red! Austria!'). The largest was planned for 24 February; the Chancellor was to give a speech before parliament, which would be broadcast by loudspeakers from every town hall in Austria. The Nazis packed Graz's main square, disrupting the broadcast, yelling slogans and singing songs, and forcing the mayor to have the Austrian flag lowered from the Town Hall and the swastika hoisted in its place. The red-white-red flag was torn to pieces by the howling crowd. This was the first time that a swastika flag flew, as it were, officially from an Austrian public building. Graz, City of the People's Insurrection.

The Graz SS had turned out in strength on the main square, still without uniforms but forming a smart, tight block. My father couldn't join them, however. He had gone from the Planner hut to Amstetten, where he wrote a petition to the President of Graz Higher Regional Court, requesting permission to practise in court in Graz. The petition was granted within days. Evidently there had long been influential elements on Graz's Higher Regional Court that sympathized with the National Socialists. But Dr Gerhard Bast, trainee attorney, never appeared in court again; higher duties awaited him.

On 9 March, three days before German troops marched into Austria, Lieutenant Colonel Erwin Remely, Regimental Commander of the 38th Regiment of the SS, stationed in Graz, promoted my father to Second Lieutenant. Thereafter he served on the staff of the regiment, which played a central part in the seizure of power in Styria, and a few months later he was appointed to the staff of Sector XXXV of the SS, Graz.

Immediately after the Anschluss, the head of the Bremen Gestapo, Erwin Schulz, was sent to Graz to set up a State Police office in the Styrian capital. Most members of the Gestapo were recruited from the existing police, but for officer positions the German chief was looking for new blood: young, energetic, politically reliable lawyers who had proved themselves in the years when the party was outlawed, impeccable National Socialists. On 20 March my father joined the Graz Gestapo; he was twenty-seven years old. He was simultaneously admitted into the SD, the Security Service of the Reichsführer of the SS. His Lower Styrian background was an asset. The acting head of the Graz Gestapo came from an old Lower Styrian family, as did the Gauhauptmann of Styria and high-ranking SS officer Armin Dadieu. The

Gestapo moved into 4 Parkring, the SD into 34 Leechgasse, and Sector XXXV of the SS, to which my father had been assigned, set up in Graz Castle.

All of a sudden he was somebody: days before, an outlawed Nazi wanted by the police, now, in the black uniform with the death's head on the cap, he was someone with real power, someone who other people in uniform saluted while they smartly clicked their heels. He only devotes a few lines of his CV to this important step:

> I was posted to the staff of 38th Regiment, Graz, on 9 March 1938 and was detailed to the SD on 20 March 1938, the same day I started working for the Secret State Police in Graz State Police office.

What led my father to make this choice, to embark on a career in the political police of the National Socialist state, an instrument of terror and horror? Why didn't he become an attorney like my grandfather? He must have known what the Gestapo was, especially in his position, with his legal training and insight into the regime's apparatus.

The Gestapo went into action immediately after the Anschluss. They conducted house searches, arrests and interrogations, acting with great brutality. Numerous people were sent to concentration camps. They were condemned without legal proceedings; all it required was a 'protective custody' warrant issued by the Gestapo, which wasn't bound by any laws. As a member of the Gestapo my father was an active participant in the regime of terror from the very start. He drew up arrest lists and interrogated people who had arbitrarily been pronounced enemies. I don't know whether he also signed protective custody warrants and beat and tortured people himself, or whether he left the torture to others (sadists, thugs, people particularly suited to such activities). I assume he was convinced that he had right on his side, that he was fighting for the right things, for the Reich of the future, the racial unity and purity of the Volk, and everything else the slogans proclaimed and many people believed, but very few of them decided on a career in the Gestapo. Why, of all people, did he? The dark shadow of this question has accompanied me for many years and I know I shall never be able to shake it off.

'Your father was an idealist; he was always decent. Everything he did was for idealistic reasons, because he believed in it. We were all idealists, we all believed,' my grandmother told me once. I was already at university and had just returned from studying in Poland. Relations were tense between us. She had known for a long time that I saw things differently, but she did not want to admit it. 'We never did anything we should be ashamed of,' she went on. 'Not your grandfather, not your father, not your uncle, not me – none of us.'

The Gestapo offered young lawyers the chance of quick promotion and good pay, prospects not easily available elsewhere. Additionally, the Secret State Police possessed unrivalled authority: it stood above the law, or rather outside all laws. The oval, silver-grey metal badge with the words 'Geheime Staatspolizei' stamped on one side and the Reich eagle with the swastika on the other conferred almost unlimited power on the bearer. 'Orders in matters of the Secret State Police are not subject to the review of the administrative courts,' the Gestapo Law of February 1936 decreed. The Gestapo was a separate state; its senior officers thought of themselves as an ideological élite, soldiers in the fight against National Socialism's internal enemies, the betrayers of the Volk – Jews, Marxists, the churches. In the SD, the Security Service of the Reichsführer of the SS, this sense of superiority was even more marked: its members felt they were the élite of the élite, answerable only to Himmler and the Führer himself. 'Henceforth, in Austria too, the Führer alone will be the supreme law and supreme arbiter of all interventions in matters of personal freedom and private property and, where necessary, of life and death,' wrote Reinhard Heydrich, the Head of the SD, about the role of the Security Service in Austria in April 1938. Originally conceived of as the party's intelligence service, after the start of the Second World War the SD increasingly became an instrument of genocide.

Members of the Gestapo were not explicitly ordered to sever their ties with organised religion, but nonetheless my father wasted no time leaving the Protestant faith. The SS questionnaire offered three options under the rubric Religious Denomination: Protestant, Catholic and *Gottgläubig*, 'Believing in God', the Nazi term for someone with religious beliefs who didn't belong to a designated religious community. 'Underline where applicable. If Believing in God, give date of leaving church.' He underlined 'Believing in God' and wrote by it, 'Yes, April 1938.' By 'Member of Lebensborn [Fount of Life]* Association' it says 'No' in his Gothic script, which has become so familiar to me in studying his life. Needless to say he was a 'Wearer of the Veterans Chevron'. You see it in any photo of him in uniform; the chevron is clearly visible on the right sleeve of his jacket.

Immediately after the Anschluss, Jews and officials of Schuschnigg's regime were arrested in Graz, as everywhere in Austria: leading representatives of Graz's Jewish community, which had 1,700 members, the Chief Rabbi David Herzog, merchants, academics, members of the liberal professions. Many were deported to Dachau or Buchenwald. Jewish businesses were publicly identified and guards posted in front of them to stop non-Jews entering. Jews were humiliated; their flats looted. On 15 March all

*SS organization that ran maternity homes for unmarried women of 'Aryan' blood who had been made pregnant by members of the SS or police. The children would be placed with SS families or in orphanages also run by the Lebensborn.

Jewish civil servants were dismissed; soon afterwards all Jewish children were expelled from state schools, and in subsequent months Jewish doctors, attorneys, vets, chemists and the like were banned from practising their respective professions. The Nazis intended to drive the Jews out of Austria. The Gestapo was responsible for putting this into practice; it drew up the lists of Jewish citizens, the observant Jews and those who had been designated *Geltungsjuden* (Jews by definition)* by the Nuremberg Race Laws. Around 2,400 people in total were targeted in Graz.

Was my father a rabid anti-Semite? I have found no evidence for it, not that that means anything; the documentation from that time is sparse and it wasn't talked about in the family. But from recent academic research on the subject, we know that not all members of the Gestapo and SD were necessarily wild anti-Semites in the Julius Streicher† mould. In fact, most of them despised this primitive form of hatred of the Jews since it belied their scientific pretensions. They considered themselves pragmatists, intellectuals: cool, detached thinkers, and thus all the more efficient when it came to implementing measures concerning the Jews, including their destruction.

In the summer of 1938 my father constantly went climbing in the mountains. He was away almost every weekend, mainly with a friend whom he called Ernstl in his journal. Mödling hut, Haindlkar hut, Buchstein hut, Planner hut. On the weekend of 23–24 July they went to Gstatterboden to climb the Tieflimauer. Things nearly went wrong on the Nordverschneidung in driving rain; a man had fallen from the rock face at the same spot not

---

*The Nuremberg Race Laws defined as Jews everyone who was descended from at least three Jewish grandparents, and everyone descended from two Jewish grandparents who belonged to the Jewish religion or was married to a Jewish person.
†Julius Streicher (1885–1946), editor from 1922 of *Der Stürmer*, a viciously anti-Semitic paper that incited the persecution of Jews and the extermination of the Jewish race. He was hanged at Nuremberg on 16 October 1946.

long before, but they got off lightly. 'Ernstl fell. Got his fingers burnt. Someone found dead,' the journal's shorthand reports, and he made a note of the dead man's name and address, as of somebody he had met somewhere and taken their details, even though he knew he would never write to them. Next to the name he drew a cross.

Someone dying in a climbing accident seemed worth mentioning to him, a tragic exception to the pleasure the mountains normally afforded. Otherwise all was well.

12

The Anschluss was greeted with less tumultuous scenes in Amstetten than in Graz. Yet there too there was a torchlight procession, swastika flags, songs – 'Raise high the flag, the ranks are closed and tight, Storm Troopers march, with firm and steady step' – elation, rejoicing. The Nazis were triumphant. To wild applause, the crutch cross flag of the Christian corporate state was hauled down from the old regional court on the main square. A solemn service of thanksgiving was held on successive Sundays in the Protestant church hall at 8 Preinsbacher Strasse, opposite my grandparents' house, to celebrate the Anschluss. A parish notice appeared in the *Amstetten Gazette* hailing the events: 'God bless our church, our people and our Führer! *Heil* Hitler!' signed Pastor Th. Beermann and Dr Rudolf Bast, Trustee.

But even these pillars of Amstetten's Protestant community, its long-serving trustee and presbyter, left the church a year later and became 'Believers in God'. They left of their own accord; no coercion was needed. My grandmother followed their example.

In 1938, in recognition of his services to the outlawed party, my grandfather was appointed Leader of the District Legal Office. There was no shortage of ardent National Socialists among the attorneys in the Lower Austrian town, but he was the staunchest. As a political leader, he was given a uniform, which he proudly wore to the Reich Party Conference in Nuremberg that year, when the ranks of Amstetten's National Socialist functionaries filed past the Führer to the strains of the 'Kaiser's Hunting March'.

'With arm thrown high, Adolf Hitler salutes the vigorous sons of his homeland. What a feeling of pride and contentment must stir in him at this unforgettable moment, now that for the first time they can march in rank and file with their comrades of like mind and like blood at the great Nuremberg gathering of the party!' wrote the *Amstetten Gazette* on 15 September 1938.

Amstetten and its environs contained only a few people who, according to National Socialist law, were not of like – namely German – blood: a handful of Jewish families, merchants and members of the liberal professions. In October 1938, as the legal representative of a builder from the small municipality of Hausmening, my grandfather instituted divorce proceedings against his client's spouse, Auguste L., at St Pölten Regional Superior Court. Auguste L. was Jewish and had remained in the Jewish religion when the couple married in 1933, which had required an official dispensation at the time. The builder had obtained authorization; perhaps his had been a great love or perhaps he had been swayed by commercial considerations: his wife was from a well-connected, prosperous Jewish family. Five years later, however, their love had evidently cooled. The association with a Jewish woman and her well-known family could no longer be of any use to him in his business or private life. In fact, the marriage now threatened to be a professional and social disaster. It cannot be a coincidence that he entrusted the divorce case to my grandfather; as Leader of the District Legal Office, he would have been well-informed on racial as well as legal issues. The petition for divorce he filed read:

The petitioner seeks the dissolution of this marriage citing the following grounds:

1. The respondent is Jewish. A marriage between an Aryan and a Jewess was not considered objectionable at the time of contraction of marriage between the parties and was further-more permitted by the Austrian authorities . . . Since the Anschluss of Austria and the German Reich and since the

introduction of the Nuremberg Laws into Austria, marriages between Aryans and Jews are expressly forbidden, however, and hence objectionable.

2. For this reason the petitioner has also become subject to an insuperable aversion for the respondent. Indeed the petitioner instantly dissolved the common household with the respondent and has since been living apart from the respondent.

3. The marriage between the contending parties can no longer accomplish the task required of it by the National Socialist State and has hence become worthless for the community as a whole.

In summary, the breakdown of the marriage due to the racial difference of the contending parties is such that the petitioner cannot be expected to continue in the marriage, nor can a restoration of a partnership in keeping with the spirit of marriage be envisaged.

The builder had been seized by an insuperable aversion to the woman with whom he had shared bed and board for years, and couldn't therefore be expected to continue the marriage. The court accepted this line of reasoning. Did my grandfather and Auguste L.'s spouse know what consequences the divorce would have for the Jewish wife? In 1938 they couldn't see the entire sequence down to its last, murderous act, but they must have known that the divorce would expose the woman to great dangers. She lost the protection that Jews married to so-called Aryans enjoyed to the end of the German Reich; she lost her social position, her property, her freedom and, finally, her life.

On 28 November 1941 Auguste L. was deported with her sister Friederike Schanzer and her sister's daughter Gertrude to Minsk, where all traces of them disappear. Of the thousand Jews who were deported on this transport from Vienna to Minsk, only a few survived. Auguste L. and her sister were not among them. The only member of the family to make his escape was a son of Friederike Schanzer, who managed to flee to Palestine. He returned to Austria after the war and later took his own life.

The builder resumed his career after 1945 as if nothing had happened. His firm flourished. There was a lot of building in the post-war years; the war – the bombing, the fighting – had caused enormous destruction across the country. Reconstruction was going to be a major undertaking; the builder was diligent and still had the right connections. Shortly after the war a master builder of this name was elected head of the local ÖVP, the Austrian People's Party, in Hausmening.

Many people seemed to have been waiting for March 1938 to break off contact with their Jewish neighbours and acquaintances; to cut them dead in public, to avoid them wherever possible. My grandparents, however, had no Jewish acquaintances whom they could ostracize or ignore. They nurtured a hatred towards Jews that had become a self-evident truth, internalized, requiring no further explanation. It was emotive, irrational. I can still hear how grandmother pronounced the word 'Jew', full of disgust, as though she were talking about dirt or vermin.

But what about Guido, the son of my grandfather's sister, who had married a Jew in Zagreb? Guido who came to Tüffer as late as 1940 to meet up with the Amstetten relatives in the Bast family house – one the Leader of the District Legal Office, the other a leading member of the Gestapo – to chat about old times, praise Aunt Pauline's nut strudel, for which the Slovenian Drolc had carefully chosen the nuts, and drink to everyone's health? There was a lot of drinking at the Basts'. It had something to do with the student fraternity. 'Guido a little hung over,' it says on the back of the photograph, which my father presumably took in 1940 in Tüffer. Cousin Guido, half Jewish, from Zagreb in Yugoslavia, which Hitler had already set his sights on in his drive to the east.

Was a member of the Gestapo allowed to share a table with a half-Jew, related or otherwise? Evidently racism did not play such a big part in the private sphere, within families, which makes it even harder to understand what happened.

The National Socialists' objective was to remove the Jews from the civil service and the professions, force them out of business and drive them out of the towns. A perverse competition developed between cities to see which could be the first to become *judenfrei*, free of Jews. Amstetten was well placed to achieve this goal ahead of most of the other towns in Lower Austria, later renamed Lower Danube (all traces of the hated name 'Austria' had to be obliterated). But first it had to dispossess its Jewish inhabitants, to 'aryanize' – or 'de-Jew', as it was called with cynical precision – their houses, flats and businesses, and to seize their assets. '*Darr Jude muss weg und sein Gerschtl bleibt da*' – dialect for 'The Jew goes and his cash stays' – was the folksy, brutal slogan coined by the Viennese edition of the *Völkischer Beobachter* in April 1938. Private citizens were given the opportunity to join in this state-sanctioned – state-decreed – pillage, with longstanding members of the party, from when it was outlawed, having the best prospects of enrichment. It became a wild free-for-all for any flats, houses and land marked down for 'de-Jewification'. Anyone who wanted a chance in the race needed an attorney who could find his way around the impenetrable maze of Nazi bureaucracy and file the necessary applications, primarily with the Property Transfer Office, which had been set up specifically for such transactions in the Ministry for Economics and Labour and decided who got the pick of the spoils.

A large proportion of the 'aryanizations' in Amstetten crossed my grandfather's desk; his brother also dealt with some aryanization matters. Any collaboration between the two of them, though, was out of the question: they had fallen out too bitterly. In September 1938 my grandfather drafted an application for Hans and Johanna Fortuna, hatters in Amstetten, for the approval of a bill of sale of a building, No. 40 Adolf-Hitler Platz in Amstetten, which was the property of the Jewish Geiduschek family:

> We are Aryans . . . We are members of the N.S.V. and N.S.D.A.P. Our son from a first marriage, Otto Schnabel, has been a member of the party since it was outlawed and is a member of the N.S.K.K. Our daughter from a first marriage, Josefa Schnabel, is a member of the N.S.D.A.P.

When Franz and Christine Köttl, master painter and wife, wanted to acquire a Jewish house in Amstetten in October 1938, they also referred to their membership of the outlawed party: 'We are German Aryans and we have both been members of the NSDAP since the prohibition years and we are also now active members of the National Socialist movement.' Drafted by my grandfather, the letter has his stamp in the top left-hand corner: 'Dr Rudolf Bast, Attorney, Amstetten, N. Ö. Preinsbacherstrasse 9. Telephone No. 218.' Although the application was warmly endorsed by Amstetten's District Party Leader, progress was slow. Six months later my grandfather tried again, this time urging a favourable response in his official capacity as Leader of the NSDAP District Legal Office. In his letter he also claimed a reimbursement of 5,000 Reichsmark on another client's behalf, from a previous aryanization case involving 'the Jews Adolf and Rosa Greger', where certain structural flaws had not been discovered initially.

> These matters are extremely pressing since the Jews' residences are urgently required.
> *Heil* Hitler!
> Leader of the District Legal Office Dr Rudolf Bast.

Stripped of their assets, Adolf and Rosa Greger were driven out of Amstetten, first to Vienna, and then, in July 1942, to Theresienstadt concentration camp and finally, two months later, to Treblinka, to the gas chambers.

The largest Jewish business in Amstetten was a fur and hide firm owned by two brothers, Hermann and Rudolf Wozasek. At the express request of the Amstetten Party District Office, the acting head of the local party, working as a liquidator, was appointed to wind up the firm in the middle of 1938. The Wozasek brothers were alleged to be 'providing moral support for the Jews in the district' and thereby hindering the smooth course of aryanization. The firm's real estate was sold, and the Wozaseks' substantial assets were swallowed up by duties and taxes, by 'Reich Flight Tax' and 'Jewish Property Tax', which were other names for state plunder. The name 'Dr Bast' appears constantly in the liquidator's accounts – Related expenses: Dr Bast 32 RM. Related expenses: Dr Bast 160 RM. Related expenses: Dr Bast 115 RM, and so on. My grandfather assisted the liquidator as legal adviser, and they both made money out of the liquidation of the Jewish firm.

The Wozasek brothers were lucky. Having been taken into protective custody in November 1938, they were released and forced to leave Amstetten for Vienna, from where they managed to escape at the last moment – one of them already had the summons for the transport to Poland in his pocket. Poland meant labour camps, Auschwitz, Treblinka and death. Hermann and Rudolf Wozasek were given the papers they needed to leave and managed to get to the USA via Switzerland and Italy. One can't tell exactly what part my grandfather played in their escape, but he undoubtedly helped Hermann Wozasek, at least, overcome official harassment and obstruction in his attempts to secure an exit permit. In November 1939, from the ship taking him to America with his wife, child and brother, Hermann Wozasek wrote a letter to the liquidator in which he thanked him for the 'goodwill' he had displayed and asked him to remember the Wozasek family fondly. He also had words of gratitude for my grandfather: 'Please convey our warmest thanks and best regards to Herr Dr Bast, who submitted an appropriate application on our behalf and thereby enabled us to leave the country.'

Was his gratitude sincere or is there a now no longer comprehensible reason for this strange-sounding letter, written on the ship between Gibraltar and Lisbon, when the Wozaseks were safely out of the Gestapo's reach? Either way, my grandfather remembered it after the war and submitted it to the People's Court Tribunal in Vienna in February 1948, when he was brought to trial for membership of the outlawed NSDAP. He argued that, as the letter from 'the Jew Hermann Wozasek' in his file showed, his work as Leader of the District Legal Office had been entirely public-spirited and selfless and devoted to national comrades in need. He had considered it his duty to help anyone who asked him for legal advice, without discrimination, including 'Social Democrats, Communists and even Jews [sic].'

After the war he wanted merely to have been a peripheral figure who had had nothing to do with the crimes of the Nazi regime. Various official agencies supported the Nazis' attempts to shuffle out of responsibility, as a note from Amstetten City Police to the People's Court Tribunal in Vienna during my grandfather's trial bears out:

Regarding: Dr Rudolf Bast . . .

The accused did not take part in any aryanization. This office also has no knowledge of anyone being denounced by him.

Historical memory can be amazingly short. Ten years becomes a long time, and erases so much from people's memories.

13

'New Planner hut in the Planner Alps. Kleiner Rotbühel, Grosser Rotbühel, Schreinl, Hintere Gollingspitze, Plannersee (torch race). Very jolly and merry.' Christmas 1938, and my father again saw in the turn of the year in the mountains 'with friends and comrades from Graz', as he noted in his journal. Perhaps they were colleagues from the Gestapo, where he worked in Department II, 'Enemy Investigation and Combat'. He became head of the department in 1939, at the age of twenty-nine. In November the same year he was appointed Government Assessor (*Regierungsassessor*) and thus was automatically promoted to SS Hauptsturmführer (Captain). One promotion entailed the other; in this respect, everything was precisely ordered. The head of the Security Police and the SD, Reinhard Heydrich, sent a note to SS Personnel Head Office under the direct control of the Reichsführer of the SS, Heinrich Himmler:

Re.: SS-U'Stuf (Second Lieutenant) Dr Gerhard Bast, SS No. 23.064.

The aforementioned has, as of 20.11, been appointed Government Assessor and is thus, under lt.RdErl.RFSSuChd-DtpoliRMdI S V 3 Nr. 72/38 v.23.6.38, to be promoted to SS Hauptsturmführer.

You are requested to draw up a letter of appointment and publish the promotion in the next SS official gazette.

The bureaucracy of terror developed a fondness for abbreviations that increasingly only the initiated could decipher, probably largely as a way to conceal the true nature of its institutions and

actions. When SS Personnel Head Office failed to respond immediately, Heydrich's office sent a second letter, upon which the letter of appointment was drafted and all the relevant departments
were notified, which involved a mass of paperwork. Even day-to-
day Gestapo business generated reams of paper; the most minor
event swelled into a complicated file that had to be submitted,
initialled and filed. This hardly fitted the image of an efficient
secret police with eyes and ears everywhere, smothering any
attempt to 'corrupt and weaken the body of the Volk' by swift,
decisive action. In practice it was often the Gestapo that was
smothered in paperwork, which in no way changed the purpose
of the organization.

In November 1939 a careless SS Unterscharführer (Corporal)
left an official briefcase in a train going from Yugoslavia to
Vienna, a catastrophe that immediately called Graz Gestapo –
specifically Dr Bast from Department II – into action. Hostile elements could conceivably have got hold of the briefcase. Dr Bast
sent a telex instructing Spielfeld Frontier Police Outpost to dispatch three officers forthwith to retrieve the briefcase, but
Spielfeld refused to accept responsibility. It had too few personnel; perhaps Vienna State Police office could do something; that
was where the train was going, after all. Dr Bast indignantly
telexed back, 'The officers are to be dispatched at once.' How they
managed it was all the same to him, but they were to dispatch 'the
relevant officers immediately, so they'll be in Vienna before the
office there gets moving. Please take note: *Heil* Hitler and dispatch. Dispatch.'

Further telexes were fired back and forth. The Leibnitz
Frontier Police Commissariat was called in, along with
Department III of the Graz Gestapo, whose head, Dr Witiska,
agreed to detach two officers to Spielfeld. Then came the news
that the briefcase had been found in the train at Bruck an der
Mur and sent on the same day to Graz station police, who,

rather than immediately submitting a report, had simply forgotten about it. A piece of sloppy work that itself called for an enquiry.

Five years later the paths of the two Graz Gestapo officers were to cross again in Slovakia. Witiska was there as the head of Einsatzgruppe (Special Task Group) H of the Security Police and the SD; my father was in charge of a Sonderkommando (Special Commando) in Witiska's area of command.

In 1939 my father again spent his leave in the mountains, staying in the Haindlkar hut in the Ennstaler Alps with a mountain guide called Gaisbauer and a woman called Käthe. He was obsessed with mountain climbing: in summer and winter, with ropes, with ice axes and crampons, with skins on his skis. Who this Käthe was I don't know; only her first name appears in the journal. He writes nothing else about her, just comments on the climbing: 'Good weather, fairly cold. Very fine and, more than anything, steady climbing, sharp rock.' Käthe may be in one of the countless photos I have of his mountaineering tours, one of the girls with hobnailed climbing boots, proper knickerbockers, cropped hair and no make-up as Nazi ideology required. At some

point she disappeared from his life, presumably without leaving any deep impression on him.

I know little or nothing of my father's private life, what he was like, how he thought. He has remained obscure to me, a figure of which I recognize only the vague outlines. He was tremendously dashing, my grandmother used to say, but this did not make the picture any clearer. He seems most recognizable to me in certain photographs, for instance in one that shows him skiing, fearlessly schussing down a steep run in the strange stance of the time, leaning low and forward. Fearless – that was another adjective grandmother liked to use on the rare occasions when she talked about him, and I strove to emulate him. I wanted to appear fearless too. I remember an episode in Oftering, when my grandfather and I were staying with a farmer who had a son a little older than me. He and I often played together in the threshing barn, which smelled wonderful from the hay stored there. High up, just under the roof, there was a diagonal brace running right across the barn, which I once crawled along on all fours – I definitely wasn't brave enough to do it standing up. When my grandfather came into the barn looking for me, he saw me above him, inching along the beam. He told me later that he stood perfectly still beneath me and didn't dare call my name. I was perhaps four or five years old at the time. I wanted to be impervious to fear, like my father.

In one photograph my father is standing in a large field, with woods in the distance. His figure is sharply defined against the cloudless sky; one can't tell what the crop is at his feet, birdsfoot trefoil or rape. He has spread his legs, clasped his hands behind his back, thrust out his jaw and fixed his gaze on the horizon. His whole form, which seems to grow out of the ground, expresses determination, toughness, detachment, brutality. Standing like that, naked and monstrously enlarged, he could pass for one of

the figures by Hitler's favourite sculptors, Josef Thorak or Arno Breker, in the Berlin Olympic Stadium in 1936. *The Victor*. I don't know whether he playfully adopted this pose for whoever took the photo or whether that is what he was really like.

My ignorance is due to the fact that I grew up in what is known as an 'intact family', that is, one with married parents and a father who was always present, always a good father to me. Presumably that prevented my mother from talking to me about my actual father or telling me anything about him, even when my second father wasn't there – according to her, that wouldn't have been proper. 'It isn't done! I don't think that's suitable!' She often used such phrases; she was given to strict moral judgements, although in other respects she was very soft and feminine.

The situation was complicated by the fact that my actual father had forced his way into my mother's marriage, alienating her, as the saying goes, from her first husband's affections. When I was born, she was still married to the man who she would marry a second time after the death of my natural father. That is why I am called by my stepfather's name, and why he is registered in all my papers, even my birth certificate, as my father. I have never found out whether he knew at the time that I was someone else's child. I only know that he was very generous to me and to my mother. He must have loved my mother above all else.

While still married to him, my mother gave birth to another man's child, an illegitimate child, which is what I was. And as she tried to find her bearings in the confused aftermath of the war, the widow of a wanted war criminal, he took her back, along with the child that was someone else's. I never felt like an illegitimate child, nor did I ever feel unwanted.

These complicated family relations contributed to the fact that nothing was ever said about anything even remotely connected to my natural father at home in Linz. It was a taboo subject. 'I'll tell you later,' my mother would say sometimes, but she never did, nor did I push her. 'It isn't done!' Was it my dead father's legacy she bequeathed to me by her silence? In the attempt to barricade herself behind those short, conventional sentences, to protect herself from unwanted familiarity and emotion, I recognize myself, a mirror image of the unknown father who vigorously thrusts out his jaw, his gaze fixed on the distance. Unapproachable. You don't show your feelings; keep them to yourself. This has become second nature to me.

Have I inherited anything from him? 'Just like his father,' my grandmother said lovingly when my mother told her that I was always getting into fights. The two women rarely met. Grandmother sometimes came to visit us in Linz, but my mother never went to Amstetten: my natural father had lived there, his parents still lived there, the town was taboo; only I was allowed to visit the place. They used to talk about me while I was still in the room, as if I wasn't there. I was a terrible brawler at my school, a private elementary school attached to the Episcopal Teachers

College in Stifterstrasse in Linz, where the teachers were all priests. When my mother reported my behaviour to my grandmother, she shook her head and laughed happily. 'Just like Gerhard,' she said.

The problems started when I got to the school in 1950. I wasn't baptized. I remember sitting with my mother in a room facing a mild-looking man with a stiff white collar who was supposed to register me. 'Religion?' he asked and without thinking started to put down Catholic. 'Believer in God,' my mother said naively. He stopped short and looked up. In those days everyone in Austria knew what that meant: the Believers in God were the Nazis, the real Nazis, not just the harmless, nominal party members. Mother smiled disarmingly at the school father. She was a beautiful woman who looked younger than her thirty-nine years and had an entrancing smile. She knew that generally she only had to break into a smile to get what she wanted. But the father wasn't going to be won over. 'That won't do, Madam,' he said stiffly, 'not here.' There was no alternative but to have me baptized; all I remember is the taste of salt on my tongue.

The teachers in Stifterstrasse were gentle and affectionate, quite unlike the usual reports you hear of clerical teachers in Catholic schools. Neither I nor, I think, any of my schoolmates was ever beaten or even made to stand in the corner. Our form teacher was a young, blond-haired man with a mild voice and soft features called Wilhelm Huber. I remember he blushed every time my mother spoke to him, which she seemed to enjoy. 'If only he weren't such a brawler,' Father Huber sometimes complained anxiously, but he was never really angry: there wasn't much else he could say about me. My mother would simply nod. After a while I used to come home every day with bruises and torn clothes. I'd be sent off neatly groomed in the morning, with a hair slide to keep my hair off my forehead (I threw that away before I got to the garden gate), and at midday I'd come back like a tramp who had been rolling around in the street. 'His father was a fighter too,' my grandmother would say.

When my stepfather came into the room, both women would fall silent. He was notably polite and correct to my grandmother, though distant. He called her 'Madam' and sketched a kiss over her hand. He was only three years younger than her. She greatly admired him and, when we were back in Amstetten and the conversation turned, as it rarely did, to my stepfather, she would say that he was a gentleman. Our house in Linz was a villa, according to her, with a wonderful garden. And the flowers: '*Gottvoll!*' And Herr Pollack: '*Ein richtiger Herr!*' ('A real gentleman!'). '*Herr*' came out very clipped, the double 'r' like a blow, when she said it. 'Impeccable manners.' Manners were very important to her. Impeccable manners and decency. 'Your father was always decent. You must never forget that,' she used to tell me.

In September 1939 Hitler invaded Poland. In the few personal and professional papers I have of my father's, the outbreak of war isn't alluded to, as if it didn't concern him. Graz was a long way from Danzig and Warsaw. Poland was crushed in a matter of weeks; people talked of a *Blitzkrieg*: it had a dashing ring to it. Einsatzgruppen, the 'Special Task Groups of the Security Police and SD', or 'Gestapo on wheels' as they were colloquially called, played an important part in the Polish campaign. Created on Hitler's orders, these units made up of members of the Gestapo, the Kripo (the Criminal Police) and the SD had already been employed in the occupations of Austria and Czechoslovakia to apprehend and eliminate 'elements hostile to the Reich'. But their main test awaited them in Poland, where they were sent in on the heels of the combat troops to clear 'hostile elements' out of the conquered areas: Reinhard Heydrich spoke of a 'comprehensive ethnic cleansing' of 'Jewry, intelligentsia, clergy and aristocracy'. The Einsatzgruppen implemented this programme with ruthless thoroughness. They were mobile assassination squads who answered not to army command but to Heydrich, Himmler and Hitler; all these three were interested in was seeing ever higher numbers of victims in the operational reports that were submitted to them.

Every officer in the Gestapo had to expect at some point to be detached to an Einsatzgruppe. A principle of strict rotation was adhered to: people were routinely transferred between Gestapo offices or sent east. No one was to spend too long in one place lest they form strong ties with the local population; everyone had to prove themselves with an Einsatzgruppe in the Volk's struggle in foreign lands.

In the spring of 1940 my father was still head of the Department for Enemy Investigation and Combat in the Graz Gestapo. The first tentative acts of resistance were occurring in Styria: bomb attacks on trains led by small groups of Austrian Slovenes. In April 1940 a bomb was planted on the track near Judenburg. Dr Gerhard Bast took charge of the case. After making enquiries and studying informers' reports, he instigated a search for a couple of men who spoke 'German with a Slavic accent'.

Before the investigation was over, he went on leave to the Tyrol, a long tour with skis through the Ötztaler Alps. Were the mountains an escape from the daily grind for him, from the grim building on the Parkring where the Graz Gestapo worked? He was on his own for the first part of his holiday. He hiked from Sölden through the Rettenbach Valley and over the Pitztalerjöchl to the Braunschweiger hut, which wasn't open, so he stayed in its winter cabin. 'Passable,' he noted in his journal. Over the next few days, still on his own, he climbed the Wildspitze, the Fernerkogel and the Mittagskogel; the Gletscher were under deep snow; on the Rettenbachjoch, he was caught in thick fog, then a snow storm got up. A week later he was joined by a friend and together they hiked from hut to hut and peak to peak until they had worked their way back to Sölden. Altogether my father was away for eighteen days, his entire year's leave. 'Perhaps the last skiing trip for a long time!' he wrote in his journal.

But he went on other trips in 1940, at least one of them official. As evidence, I have a dozen photographs of Italian scenes: Ostia; Roman ruins with pines in the distance and a man in German uniform in the foreground; a palace in the monstrous fascist style, presumably in Rome, at the foot of which stand black guards wearing picturesque turbans, white trousers and full capes, holding lances with pennants; there are more of the same sort of guards, Abyssinians in operetta costumes, in the passageways of the palace. In another picture a group of uniformed men, SS perhaps, are crowded onto a terrace looking at the Italian landscape: *Bildungsbürger*, German middle-class intellectuals in uniform on a visit to their Italian allies – half holiday, half work. Only one of the photographs is puzzling. It has 'Šibenik 1940' written on the back, but Šibenik is in Dalmatia, which was still a part of Yugoslavia in 1940. It seems hard to imagine that a group of SS officers in uniform would have been able to pay a visit to Yugoslavia at that point.

I know that he returned to Yugoslavia that year, and again photographs are the only trace I have of this trip to Gottschee and Tüffer, the places of his childhood. This time he met his cousin Guido and then moved on to Zagreb, Sarajevo and Belgrade. I have a whole stack of photos of typical tourist scenes, such as the Ban Jelačić statue and the market in front of it in Zagreb. Judging by the heavy clothes of the women stallholders and the passersby, coupled with the lack of snow, it must be early spring or the start of winter. Another picture shows an inconspicuous house with a garden in what looks like a fairly poor suburb, although the street in front of the house is tarmacked. On the back it says 'Vrhovec 41'. According to family lore, grandfather's sister Käthe owned a property in Vrhovec, a suburb of Zagreb, which she had presumably acquired by marriage. As she was childless, the property, probably just a one-storey house with a garden, went after her death to her sister's son, Guido, who is in the picture taken in Laško. So Vrhovec 41 should be Guido's home. Perhaps father stayed there with his half-Jewish cousin while he was in Zagreb. The weather must have been rainy in Belgrade: there are hardly any passers-by to be seen on the streets; everything looks grey and damp. *Beograd, Prestol trg. Beograd, Kralja Aleksandra.* It is striking that he captioned the pictures in Serbo-Croat rather than German, just as he always wrote Laško and Kočevje, never Tüffer and Gottschee. He must have been able to speak a few words of Slovenian – he was there often enough – but under 'Foreign Languages' in the SS questionnaire in his file he has put 'None'.

What did he do on this trip? It can't have been a holiday; he had already used up his leave in the Tyrolean mountains. That leaves only one possibility: in 1940 a striking number of German tourists were travelling round Yugoslavia, all youngish men in civilian clothes with a military snap in their haircuts, their bearing, their brisk manner. All had cameras and photographed whatever they could: bridges, train stations, factories and other subjects that might be of military interest, to the air force for instance. Yugoslav police and counterintelligence knew exactly what these men were doing, but they couldn't take any action against them: relations between the Kingdom of Yugoslavia and Hitler's Germany were officially good, even if they didn't trust the Germans an inch.

So this was an espionage trip. Either for the SD, which had its own foreign service, or perhaps military intelligence 'borrowed' the Graz Gestapo officer, if such a thing were possible given the rivalry between the two organizations. I don't know whether officers were recruited or volunteered in such cases. As a Lower Styrian by birth with relatives in Slovenia and Croatia, my father would have been ideal for such a mission. He could have used it as an opportunity to visit his friends and relatives in Yugoslavia, or else they could have served as cover for his activities. All the photos I have found in his papers are tourist shots – heavily veiled women in Sarajevo, streetscapes, buildings, market scenes; I suppose he would have handed over any pictures of military significance. Perhaps he met agents as well, in Gottschee, Tüffer and Zagreb. There were still enough members of the German minority in Yugoslavia who longed for the German Reich. In any event, it seems probable that the aim of this trip was to acquire information that would be of use in preparations for an attack on Yugoslavia.

14

In the early morning of 6 April 1941 the German Luftwaffe flew its first sorties against the Yugoslav capital without war having been declared. Six hundred and eleven planes dropped 440 tonnes of bombs on Belgrade; 2,000 people died in two days. On 9 April German troops occupied the border town of Maribor; Slovenia was conquered in three days without any serious resistance. The former territories of Lower Styria and Upper Carniola, without the latter's capital Ljubljana, fell to the German Reich. Italy was awarded Ljubljana and Lower Carniola, and their ally Hungary was granted the eastern part of the province, the Upper Mür region.

On 12 April the Gauleiter of Styria, Siegfried Uiberreither, travelled to Maribor, now called by its German name of Marburg again, and announced a 'Germanization of the province' and attendant expulsion of unwanted Slovenes. 'We want to bind this land so tightly that there's only room for the German, and for those Styrians who have fought loyally and in comradely fashion shoulder to shoulder with our national comrades for years and decades and centuries . . . And I make no secret of it, my national comrades, everyone else must go! We will implement the necessary measures with steely composure . . .'

Lower Styria was forcibly annexed to Styria; orders were given to deport around 260,000 Slovenes, a third of its population, and important duties were assigned to the Gestapo and SD, which set up branch offices in Marburg. These answered to Gestapo and SD headquarters in Graz, where, even before the invasion, information about Lower Styria and its 'anti-German elements' had been zealously collected. Using previously established lists, a string of people were arrested immediately after the occupation, including many Slovenian intellectuals and priests. A great deal of this information came from Graz Gestapo's Department of Enemy Investigation and Combat, under the command of Dr Gerhard Bast. He may have already been compiling names on his Yugoslav trip the year before. I don't know whether my father went to Lower Styria at this point, but his younger brother, Helmut Bast, my uncle Helmut, certainly did. He took over an SD branch office in a small place called Gornji Grad (Oberburg in German) between Celje and Ljubljana.

The two brothers' careers present obvious parallels. Both studied law in Graz, joined the Germania duelling fraternity, sported their duelling scars with pride, espoused German nationalist views and became radical National Socialists. The younger brother, who was born in Amstetten in 1914, applied for the SS like the older. In official documents from 1941 onwards he is referred to as an SS candidate member and acting head of the SD's branch office in Oberburg. Part of his job was to decide which Slovenian families should be expelled, which individual Slovenes should be arrested and which, more rarely, should be released.

On 14 May 1941 he sent an express letter to the Secret State Police branch office in Marburg about the examination of protective detainee Cerin Iwan, who was born on 10 February 1884:

> For reasons of general security I am opposed to the release of the aforementioned prisoner. Cerin Iwan is known in the municipality of Prassberg as an enemy of Germany and his attitude is very hostile to everything German. This is apparent in the upbringing of his whole family and in particular of his illegitimate son Divjak Iwan, who is dealt with below . . . If resettlement is to be proceeded with, then the whole family should be removed.
>
> Dr Helmut Bast, Acting Head of SD Branch Office.

I found out by chance that my father's younger brother had been in the SD. My discovery was the result of a mix-up. In response to an enquiry, I was issued with documents in the Slovenian State Archives in Ljubljana, which mentioned a Dr Bast, who was working in 1941 in Oberburg. At first I thought it was my father. But he was with the Graz Gestapo at that time, and he wasn't a mere SS candidate either but an SS Hauptsturm-führer. My uncle eventually joined the paratroopers rather than the SS, for reasons unknown to me – perhaps his severe short-sightedness made him ineligible for the SS; his career in the SD ended at that point as well. But I still wasn't surprised to find out that he had worked for the SD for at least a few months, and in occupied Slovenia for good measure; nor that the woman he was married to at the time was employed by the terror apparatus as a typist for the chief of the Security Police and the SD in Marburg.

It is hard to reconstruct the service records of members of the Gestapo and the SD in full detail. Documents are scattered between archives and many have been lost or destroyed for fear of prosecution by the people they implicate. At some point in the summer of 1940 my father was sent to Germany, which was then called the Old Reich, and stationed for a time in Coblenz. This emerges from a memo sent by Coblenz State Police office to SS personnel files in August 1940 reporting that Hauptsturm-führer Dr Gerhard Bast, Government Assessor by profession, had obtained the Bronze Reich Sports Badge on 24 June 1940; even the number of the award certificate is given. Probably attached to SD Head Office in Berlin during this period, he may have undergone some sort of training while serving in the Coblenz Gestapo. After all, he was a qualified lawyer with no previous police experience.

I discovered something else in the papers from his time in Coblenz: a postcard from the German Consulate General in

Trieste to Amstetten NSDAP District Headquarters, Legal Office, saying, 'Your communication of the 14th of this month to the Embassy in Rome concerning the procurement of records from Treviso Province has been forwarded for reasons of jurisdiction to the German Consulate in Venice.' The card is postmarked Berlin; it was probably sent there by courier and then forwarded to Amstetten, to my grandfather, Leader of the Legal Office.

The records it refers to were presumably needed for compiling my father's SS genealogical table, which had to comply with even more exacting standards than those expected of normal party members. SS men had to prove Aryan extraction extending back to the eighteenth century. The fact that people still burdened offices and institutions in the middle of the war with such tasks – my father wasn't the only one searching for his ancestors; tens of thousands of people in Germany and Austria kept parishes, registry offices and consulates in neighbouring provinces busy with similar enquiries – illustrates a mad characteristic of the system.

In January 1941 my father was back in the Ostmark (the official name for Austria), in Linz, where this time he was awarded the Bronze SA Sports Badge. The memo notifying the SS Personnel Office gives his profession as 'Government Assessor, currently chief of the Linz State Police office.' This was quite a career leap; he had joined the Gestapo less than three years before. He was only acting head, though; Humbert Achamer-Pifrader was temporarily drafted away from Linz, but returned to hold the post until March 1941.

Linz enjoyed a privileged position in the Third Reich as 'The Führer's Home Town' (Hitler had famously attended the *Realschule* [secondary school] in Linz for four years), which far outstripped the city's actual significance. A posting to Linz was therefore a special honour. The Linz State Police office, which

115

had a staff of around fifty, occupied the requisitioned Kolping-haus, the Catholic Young Working Men's hostel. The SD had its offices in a villa, 4 Auf der Gugl, on a hill above the town, two or three minutes' walk from the house in which my mother lived.

I assume that my father already knew her then, at the start of 1941. My stepfather had nothing to do with the Gestapo or the SS, but nor was he just a nominal party member. He knew Hitler from *Realschule* in Linz; he was two years younger than the future Führer, but only a year below him, since Hitler had had to repeat a year. A recurrent name in his school reports is that of the history and geography teacher Leopold Poetsch, an ardent German nationalist who Hitler himself said had played an important role in forming his thinking. Poetsch taught my stepfather from his first to his fourth year, when, unlike Hitler, he got consistently good grades: 'Commendable' (for moral conduct) and 'Excellent' (for progress). Later the two met again. Hitler's vivacious niece, Geli Raubal, had a number of admirers in Linz and my stepfather was one of them. By his own account, my stepfather once asked Hitler for his ward's hand in marriage in the 1920s. Hitler turned him down, which he found mortifying, but this did not prevent him becoming an enthusiastic advocate of Hitler's ideas. In September 1940 he was appointed to Linz's Advisory Committee for the Fine Arts by the *Gauhaupstadt*'s Chief Burgomeister; a year later his duties were extended and he was made Honorary Representative for the Fine Arts on the Municipal Board of Culture. Considering that Hitler wanted to turn the city on the Danube into an international art metropolis, this was a presti-gious appointment, even if it carried no real powers. After the war my stepfather's pension was docked as punishment for holding this post.

It is conceivable that my stepfather, father and mother could have come across one another on any number of official occa-sions. Or perhaps my father met her by chance, strolling in the park in the fashionable Bauernberg residential district where she used to walk her German shepherd with the very un-German name of King. King, incidentally, was requisitioned by the Wehrmacht towards the end of the war – possibly to be drafted into some sort of Home Guard Dog Brigade or to be trained to harass any invading army behind the lines. The animal was never found after 1945; it was never revealed whether he had died or found a new owner. There was a lot of talk about King at home after the war, about what a paragon of beauty, cleverness and loyalty he was. I have a portrait of my mother painted by my stepfather in the 1930s in the *Neue Sachlichkeit* style, a small picture, 20 by 25 cm, which only shows her face. It is the remains of a full-length portrait, which apparently showed the magnificent German shepherd loyally sleeping at her feet. The oil painting was in the house when it was hit by a bomb in December 1944: all of it was burnt except my mother's face.

The Gestapo's field of duties was almost incalculably broad. Besides supervising the so-called 'aliens' – foreign workers, forced labourers, prisoners of war – who were employed in factories and on farms, their job was to spy on the German Volk itself. They had to detect all forms of organized resistance, by Communists, Social Democrats or Christian religious communities, and private intractability towards the regime. Grousing and grumbling, as it was known, came under the Treachery Act and could be punished with prison or 'protective custody', which often meant being sent to a concentration camp for an indefinite period. Other matters dealt with by the Gestapo included 'Intentional Listening to Enemy Radio Broadcasts', 'Demoralization of the Troops', 'Damage to Military Resources (Sabotage)', contraventions of the Nuremberg Race Laws, and much else besides. At the start of 1941 there were almost no Jews left in Linz and the Upper Danube, as Upper Austria was now called. Most had already been driven out.

The few who had managed to evade expulsion were for the most part in what were known as 'Privileged Mixed Marriages' – that is, married to an Aryan partner who resisted official pressure to dissolve the marriage.

'There is reason,' wrote the acting chief of the Linz Gestapo, Dr Gerhard Bast, on 30 January 1941, 'to devote more attention to the surveillance of Jews living in the *Reichsgau* Upper Danube than has recently been the case.' Curfew exemptions could only be granted by the Gestapo, he continued. As much information as possible was to be gathered about the Jews and Jewish *Mischlinge** still living in Upper Danube: had they adopted the first names of Israel and Sara as prescribed by law; did they possess identity cards and, if so, which; did they own their dwellings or were they tenants cohabiting with an Aryan; were they still telephone and radio subscribers and did they belong to the Jewish faith or had they converted to another (if so, which)? In addition, the Gestapo required all the particulars of Jews in mixed marriages, the places of residence of any children of such marriages and notification as to whether the husband and/or the sons had joined the army.

The point of this endless catalogue of questions was to intimidate the partners of Jews in so-called 'Protected Marriages' into getting a divorce. The *Führergau* Upper Danube had to be rendered completely *judenrein*, 'cleansed of Jews'.

I remember Linz in the 1950s and 1960s as a city without Jews. Perhaps there were a few, there must have been, but we never noticed them, apart from one. There was a sweet shop in Linz at that time called the Zuckerl Schwager. It wasn't on my way to

---

*A category created by the Nuremberg Race Laws, *Mischlinge* comprised all people with two Jewish grandparents, 'half Jews', who did not belong to the Jewish religion and were not married to a Jewish person (the so-called *Mischlinge* of the first degree) and all people with one Jewish grandparent, 'quarter Jews' (*Mischlinge* of second degree).

school, but I knew of it, not least because the name used to come up at home when for one reason or another Jews were the subjects of conversation. The shop's owners were said to be Jewish. My stepfather, otherwise a refined, very reserved man, used to grimace spitefully and say 'Zuckerl Schwager' in what he thought was a Yiddish accent. It came out sounding roughly like 'Zickerl Schwager'. The shop didn't look very prepossessing from the outside; it seemed old-fashioned, archaic even, as did the sweets in the window – or was I just projecting onto the display what I had heard at home? I remember people saying that the doughnuts at Schwager's tasted horrible. I never tried them myself, because we never shopped there.

It was only later that my brother and I rebelled against the casual anti-Jewish remarks at home, entering into heated arguments that my mother called 'unedifying'. She always tried to preserve harmony, to smooth things over; when a row was looming, she would try to change the subject to something harmless. But it didn't do much good. We were young and inconsiderate; we could have sustained those quarrels for hours, days even. My stepfather mainly cut short the battle of words by silently getting to his feet and leaving the table. I still admire the fact that he did not bear a grudge. We often hurt him deliberately, but he never let us see it, and in a way he never tried to force his point of view on us. At some point, both sides gave up – we lost our burning enthusiasm for those quarrels and he avoided making insensitive remarks.

I don't know how long my father worked for the Gestapo in Linz. At any rate he was back at the State Police office in Coblenz in June 1941. He was appointed Government Counsellor (*Regierungsrat*) the same month.

I issue this warrant of commission in the full expectation that the appointee will conscientiously perform the duties of his office in keeping with his oath of service and justify the trust invested in him by this appointment. I also hereby assure him of my personal protection.

The Führer, Adolf Hitler.

15

Six months later my father rose a rank in the SS as well and was promoted to Sturmbannführer, the equivalent of a major in the Wehrmacht. In the middle of July 1941 he was transferred from Coblenz to Münster, the capital of *Gau* North Westphalia, to be the deputy chief of the local Gestapo. Münster's was a large Gestapo HQ with about 120 officers (fifty were employed in Coblenz and Linz respectively), whose area of responsibility covered the administrative districts of Münster, Minden and Osnabrück, as well as the provinces of Lippe and Schaumburg-Lippe.

There was a concrete reason why the Gestapo office in Münster was so heavily staffed at a time when the institution was complaining of personnel shortages everywhere else: Münster was a centre of Catholic resistance, which neither the party nor the normal police could cope with on their own. In Clemens August Graf von Galen, Bishop of Münster since 1933, the National Socialists had found an implacable adversary who refused to keep his peace. The bishop called upon the church actively to oppose National Socialism and set a courageous example himself. When the Pope addressed the position of the Catholic Church in the German Reich and sharply criticized the National Socialist regime in the encyclical 'With Burning Anxiety' in March 1937, the Bishop of Münster ensured that the Pope's message was immediately broadcast through his diocese. In 1941 the turbulent priest, known by the faithful as the 'Lion of Münster' for his courage, delivered three sermons denouncing the Gestapo's hostility to the Church and the Nazis' practice of euthanasia, the state-decreed murder of the mentally ill and handicapped. In one sermon the bishop publicly called those responsible for the euthanasia murderers.

The bishop's sermons, read out in all the churches in Münster, caused great indignation among the town's inhabitants; copies were circulated throughout Germany and even reached the front. The Gestapo were at a loss: the bishop was so popular they didn't dare touch him.

It was different with the Jews. No voices of protest were raised on their behalf. Since the summer of 1939 the Jews of Münster had lived crowded together in fourteen so-called Jews' Houses, which made their persecution easier. In December 1941 the Gestapo began deporting German Jews to the east. At first they were deported to Riga, Minsk and the Lublin area, where they were shot on the spot or put into work camps, which were in practice extermination camps. On 25 October 1941 the chief of the Secret State Police, Heinrich Müller, informed all subordinate departmental offices that henceforth all emigration of Jews was to be prevented, apart from by deportation to the east by the Gestapo in what, in official parlance, were called 'evacuation measures' to conceal their true purpose.

Everything was planned down to the smallest detail. Departmental Section IV B 4 of the Reich Security Main Office under Adolf Eichmann informed the respective State Police offices when a transport was to leave, where it was going and how many people it was to contain. The Gestapo then drew up an organizational plan establishing the precise sequence of formalities to be observed prior to the transport's departure. Lists of the Jews to be deported were compiled and the relevant offices, district and local police authorities, district administrators and mayors notified. Then Reich Railway management was informed when and where the Jews were to be entrained, how much rolling stock – third-class coaches (for the Jews) and second-class coaches (for the escort detachment of *Schutzpolizei* [Protection Police]) – was needed, when the transport was to leave and when it was to reach its destination. Nothing was left to chance.

On 30 October 1941 the Münster Gestapo instructed the relevant district authorities to compile a list of Jews still resident in their area. On 18 November Münster Gestapo issued the first orders for the evacuation of around 400 Jews from the Münster region; 200 were to be added in Osnabrück and a further 400 in Bielefeld. A set of instructions painstakingly listed what the Jews were obliged to take with them on the journey and what was strictly prohibited:

In order to register the Jews' total assets, every Jew (including children and wives) has to fill out the enclosed Assets' Declaration neatly and accurately in duplicate. Not to be lasted [*sic*] are any objects the Jews will be taking with them when they are evacuated.

Each person must take:

Means of payment of up to RM 50, in Reich Credit notes. A suitcase with items of equipment (no bulky goods). A complete set of clothing (sturdy footwear). Bedding with blanket. Food for 3 weeks (bread, flour, pearl barley, beans). Kitchen utensils (plate or pot) with spoon.

Prohibited items:

Shares, foreign currency, savings deposit books etc. Valuables of any sort (gold, silver, platinum – except wedding rings). Livestock. Food-ration cards (these are to be confiscated and handed over to the nearest branch of the Ministry of Economics against a receipt). Shares, certificates and contracts relating to Jewish assets are to be added to the Assets' Declaration, when the relevant documents can be produced.

Cash and valuables (jewellery and so on) are to be confiscated by the officials who fetch the Jews from their dwellings and listed on the attached receipt form. The receipt will be signed by the Jew and the official and kept with the cash in an envelope. This is also to be added to the Assets' Declaration. The sum of RM 50 to be taken by each person should not be included in the receipt, but should be collected and given to the transport leader when the Jews are handed over in Münster. To ensure everyone has these funds when the transport leaves, there can be no objection to officials taking cash from wealthy Jews, who are likewise to be deported, and giving it to Jews of limited means.

On the day of the transport the dwelling is attended to (water and gas turned off, front door locked and sealed). No inventory. The hand luggage to be taken by the Jews must not weigh more than 50 kg.

Further, it should be left to each individual Jew's discretion whether to bring: mattresses, woollen blankets (no eiderdowns or quilts), iron stoves, tools (spade, hoe etc.), 1 cooking pot, 1 wash basin & 1 bucket and a small amount of soap. Knife, fork and shaving utensils are not to be taken.

Sufficient provisions for 3 weeks are to be provided for the Jews by the Food Office.

The Jews are to be handed over on 11.12.1941 in the morning in Münster, Warendorferstr. at the Gertrudenhof Inn.

The document was signed by Dr Bast, my father. He personally supervised the rounding up of the Jews and their being taken to the Gertrudenhof, where they and their bags were meticulously searched. The Gertrudenhof was a popular holidaymakers' restaurant with a beer garden, not far from Gestapo headquarters in Gutenbergstrasse. The Gestapo requisitioned it on 11 and 12 December; the owners had to stay on the first floor. The next day the Jews were taken to the station and herded into the waiting carriages. A survivor, Siegfried Weinberg, remembers them being cursed and beaten, especially the older ones. From a report of the time, it is clear that Dr Bast also supervised the Jews being ferried to the station and loaded onto the train. Allowing them to take tools and stoves was meant to give the victims the impression that they genuinely were being sent east on work detail.

When the Jews arrived in Riga after travelling for three days, they were herded into the ghetto where shortly before 26,000 Latvian Jews had been shot to make way for the newcomers. They found a scene of devastation: kicked-in doors, smashed furniture, torn bits of clothing, traces of blood everywhere. Here and there half-empty plates stood on tables, pots on the stove; the food had frozen. From November 1941 to February 1942 a total of 20,000 German, Austrian and Czech Jews were deported to Riga. Only a few survived.

Did my father know what would happen to the Jews he sent to Riga? A young Jew who was unexpectedly released from a transport in Bielefeld in the summer of 1942 told how he went to the station to pick up his luggage, which had been stored there. A young Gestapo official chased him away saying, 'Clear off, boy, otherwise you'll be on your way up the chimney too!'

My father was no young Gestapo official. Granted he was only thirty, but he was already deputy chief of a large Gestapo bureau, where important information was pooled. He knew about everything in his position, including what was happening in the east.

A week after the first transport, the planning for the next one began. In a circular, the Münster Gestapo informed the district administrators and Chief Burgomeisters of its area that a transport of Jews from Dortmund was to be sent east in January 1942. 'Münster State Police office has been asked to provide 500 Jews for this transport from the industrial region. As it will not in all probability be possible to meet this figure, I request you provide names of the Jews still living in this region who can be part of this transport . . .'

Riga was again the destination. Münster Gestapo's deputy chief, Dr Bast, was once more involved in the preparations for the transport, but this time somebody else had to supervise the rounding up of the Jews and their transport to the station, because in January 1942 my father went on an SS skiing course in the Riesengebirge in the Sudetenland. The SS had its own ski hut in the Riesengebirge, in Langenberg bei Petzer under the Schneekoppe mountain. The little town of Petzer is today in the Czech Republic and is called Pec pod Snezkou. From 10 to 26 January two dozen members of the SS were taught the rudiments of skiing by experts from among their ranks. My father, an out-standing skier, acted as one of the instructors.

'Day 1: Walking, pole holding, holding between thumb and forefinger, walking with poles, without poles . . . Day 2: Repeat of Day 1. Plough, skis in V, no edging . . .' he noted in his journal. I have a whole series of snapshots of the skiing course in Riesengebirge, which, judging from the variety of formats, were taken by different people. A row of men in the snow smartly lined up in front of the ski instructor, almost all in plain clothes. Group photos in front of a snow-encrusted mast (on a peak?), before the start of a downhill race, in front of the SS ski hut – a crowd of suntanned men, mostly in baggy plus fours, some with gaiters, a few with cameras round their neck, looking like archetypal men of the time on holiday. One photo shows the inside of the spacious hut; 'Riesengebirge '42. Social evening, SS ski hut,' it says on the back. Men no longer in their first youth in ski jumpers and shirts are sitting in a big hall, staring earnestly into their beer mugs; no one is laughing. There are a couple of women as well and a portrait of the Reichsführer of the SS and Head of the German Police, Heinrich Himmler, looks down on his troops from one wall. 'Weather mainly beautiful, very cold. Snow grand throughout. SS hut grand, food good,' my father summed up the fortnight in the Riesengebirge.

As the Jews who were being deported to Riga on the Dortmund transport left Münster on 27 January, my father was already on his way home from Riesengebirge to Amstetten, where he spent a few days with his parents. There the news reached him that he had been awarded the NSDAP Bronze Long Service Medal by the Führer on 30 January. At the start of February he went to Garmisch-Partenkirchen for SS shooting practice. A picture shows him in uniform kneeling in the snow, his rifle propped on his crossed ski poles; other uniformed figures are lying beside him, shooting at a target that is out of the picture. Skis and poles are scattered in the snow, and in the background the Kramer massif towers up into the clear winter sky. Members of the Gestapo had to be able to do more than just write reports and supervise transports. The scene is like one of those images of biathlons you see on television. Just under three weeks later, my father was back in Münster. A third transport of around 400 Jews was dispatched from Münster's area of activity, this time to

Lublin. The people were herded into ghettos in Lublin and the neighbouring towns, where the conditions were horrific; many starved or froze to death in the first weeks; anyone who couldn't work was shot on the spot.

On 11 June 1942 the twenty-seven-year-old Polish forced labourer Polykarp Raczynski was hanged in the picturesque little Westphalian town of Oelde. Raczynski had spent some time in Oelde police prison, for reasons that were later of no interest to anyone, and while trying to escape had dealt a police sergeant a blow to the skull with an iron window bar that had wounded him seriously. Before the hanging, the sentence was read out to Raczynski in Polish by an interpreter from the Münster Gestapo; there was no priest present, only a few Gestapo officials. The senior officer who gave the execution order was, according to the police surgeon in attendance, a man who used Austrian dialect, 'Leading me to believe that it must have been Government Counsellor Dr Bast.'

The surveillance and prosecution of foreign forced labourers – civilian and prisoners of war – was one of the Gestapo's key tasks, especially if the 'aliens' were guilty of a criminal offence, which, given the repressive laws, did not require much. The foreign workers were removed from German jurisdiction and put in the Gestapo's charge, which was police, judge and jury to them. How they were treated depended on where they were from: a Frenchman would be dealt with considerably more leniently than a Pole or Russian. Among the offences most regularly punished by the Gestapo were theft (it could be a handful of potatoes or a few half-rotten swedes), so-called 'Breaches of Contracts of Employment' (these included any unauthorized absence from the workplace, which was generally punished by 'Labour Education Camp' or concentration camp) and intimate relations with German women. If a French civilian worker got involved with a

German girl, he could escape with a stern reprimand, perhaps a few weeks' detention. If the worker was a member of the so-called 'Eastern Peoples', a Pole, Russian or Ukrainian, he would end up in a concentration camp or on the gallows. It was not easy for the ordinary citizen to tell who was considered a member of an alien race and who wasn't, so guidelines were produced.

Related to us and therefore not alien are members of the following Germanic peoples: Flemish, Dutch, Danish, Norwegian, Swedish. All others with the exception of the Swiss are alien.

Of the alien peoples, the Italians, Hungarians, Croats, Rumanians and Bulgarians are our allies. All others are members of enemy states.

Affairs between German women and members of non-allied 'Eastern peoples' were prosecuted with especial zeal on the express order of Himmler, who feared a 'racial befouling of the body of the German Volk'. Only in exceptional cases, if they were considered *eindeutschungsfähig* ('Germanizable'), did the accused escape with their lives. Potential candidates were photographed by the Gestapo's Records Office and their racial characteristics were strictly examined and measured. For them, Germanization in practice meant being immediately drafted into the Wehrmacht.

In 1942 a number of forced labourers were sentenced to death for various offences by Münster Gestapo and, on confirmation of their sentences, executed by the RSHA. The hangings were performed with a so-called 'trap table', which was set up under a balcony to which a rope was attached. The folding trap table was kept in the Anatomy Institute at Münster University and when required taken to the place of execution and assembled there. A hinged leaf in the table was operated by a lever; the prisoner fell and was strangled. Where possible the hangings took place near the scene of the crime, and several Gestapo officials were detailed to attend to make sure everything went smoothly; spiritual care was not provided.

'Dr Bast,' a former Gestapo official from Münster told the investigating judge after the war, 'attended almost every hanging and often supervised them as well, including ones at which I was not present. I got the impression that Dr Bast, who liked to brag generally and was always banging the pan-German drum, enjoyed the hangings and took pleasure in taking part in them.'

As hangmen the Gestapo used Polish civilian workers who had been arrested for minor offences and adjudged 'Germanizable'. The office of hangman was clearly a racial test: whoever displayed the necessary hardness or brutality had made some progress towards being accepted. There was apparently no shortage of candidates. Hanging was never mentioned in correspondence between the Reich Security Main Office in Berlin and the Gestapo offices, only 'special handling', a euphemism that was also used for the mass murder of the Jews.

When members of the Münster Gestapo were examined by an investigating judge in the 1960s about events in their office, they all said that they hadn't thought the hangings of the Poles were right, but that they couldn't avoid taking part because the orders had come from their superiors. And if their superiors gave an order, it was carried out. One of the officials, a gardener in civilian life, explained that, after all, both the Münster Gestapo and the RSHA in Berlin had sets of 'fully qualified lawyers who looked into the individual cases. Lawyers have to know the legal way to deal with a case. So, as an assistant, I didn't worry about it.'

One of these fully qualified lawyers was my father. His former subordinates in Münster had graphically different memories of the deputy chief with the Austrian accent. One remembered a 'completely mad dog, who was always shouting'. Another described him to the investigating magistrate as a 'comradely and generous person' who hadn't struck him as unpleasant.

Mind you, he conceded, he had hardly had any contact with Dr Bast professionally. Dr Bast, said a third, was a 'sportsman who spent his every free moment playing handball'. He had not impressed him as a particularly forceful character. Others had absolutely no memory of an Austrian in Münster Gestapo HQ, which is surprising given that my father's successor was also from Austria.

A week after Raczynski's execution, the Pole Michal Katarzynski was hanged in the little town of Lippramsdorf bei Haltern. He was alleged to have had both a relationship with a married German woman and stolen food from his employer to give to her. The death of Katarzynski is recorded in the register of deaths in Haltern's registry office, without a cause of death. Whether Dr Bast attended the hanging is not known. It is only recorded that, after the hanging, the Polish forced labourers living in the area were marched past the hanged man on the Gestapo's orders. The execution of their compatriot was to serve as a warning to them. Staff members of Münster Anatomy Institute then folded up the trap table and stowed it away in an estate car along with the body, which ended up on the Institute's dissecting table.

At least seven Polish forced labourers were hanged during my father's time in Münster. It is impossible to find out the exact number, since most of the relevant documents were destroyed at the end of the war. One former Münster Gestapo officer recounted how he was entrusted with the task of burning incriminating material in the spring of 1945. He said that he spent two or three days burning files on the concrete roof of Gestapo HQ in Gutenbergstrasse.

In 1942 my father travelled to Gottschee with my mother. I have two photographs from the trip in front of me. They show my mother and father (they have clearly each taken the other's photo) standing in a field; there are houses in a hollow in the background which are presumably part of Gottschee town. 'Kočevje '42' is written on the back of one of the pictures in my father's writing. It was unusual, to say the least, for a senior Gestapo official – even more so for one from Lower Styria himself – to choose the Slovenian name rather than the German one.

When the two snapshots were taken, whether it was spring, summer or autumn, is hard to say; the trees in the background are too far away to tell the season from their foliage. In any event it wasn't high summer or deep winter: my mother is wearing a twin-set jacket and my father a light trench coat over a dark three-piece suit. He smiles self-confidently into the camera, his head tilted to one side; the picture is slightly blurred so that you can't see the scars on his chin and left cheek. My mother has a hint of a smile as well, but there is a wary uncertainty to her expression as if she weren't sure what to think of a situation that must have been extremely complicated. In the photos they look like a couple on honeymoon. My mother's hair is freshly waved and she has a dress handkerchief in the breast pocket of her light jacket and a flat handbag wedged under her right arm. She looks

very young, much younger than him, although there wasn't much more than a year between them. He was thirty-one at the time, and she had a husband and two children in Linz, the younger of whom, my half-brother, was born in August 1942. I don't know whether this was before or after the trip to Kočevje, but she appears girlishly slim in the photograph, which suggests that they went some time after my half-brother's birth, perhaps in late autumn, at the end of October, start of November. In which case, where did she leave the baby? At home, with the nanny and her husband? At least as puzzling is the question of why the two of them went to Gottschee – or Kočevje, as he wrote – at all at that time.

The German invaders had ceded Gottschee, along with Lower Carniola and its capital Ljubljana, to Italy in May 1941, although naturally without the native 'Gottscheer' Germans. These had been ordered by Hitler to resettle in another area, the so-called Ranner Triangle in the south-eastern tip of Lower Styria, which comprised three towns, Rann, Gurkfeld and Lichtenwald, from which all the Slovenian inhabitants had been expelled. By 1942 Gottschee, sparsely enough populated to begin with, was almost deserted, a place where the Yugoslav partisans deployed and withdrew to when the Italians mounted one of their half-hearted operations. The few Gottscheer who had not answered the call to resettle, perhaps 400 or 500 out of a total of 12,000, had fled from the partisans to the larger settlements, primarily the town of Gottschee, where the Italian occupiers had a garrison. In the spring of 1942 large parts of the Italian Provincia di Lubiana were firmly in the hands of the partisans, who went so far as to issue the population with passes. The Italians made only sporadic attempts to re-establish control in small areas outside the towns.

To go to Gottschee at this time was more than just adventurous, especially accompanied by a woman. Then there's the question of whether the two of them had permission to be in the area at all. My father carried the red ID card of the Security Police and SD, which opened many doors (and perhaps border crossings), but my mother was a housewife from Linz who certainly had no business in what was officially a bandit area. I don't know whether he was there on assignment (though his office was in Münster) or whether this was nostalgia, a chance to show his lover the landscape of his early childhood and the scene later of so many hunting trips. I wonder whether they visited one of his childhood friends, a German who had decided to stay or to return (people did that too), or a Slovenian acquaintance who saw no harm in being seen with a member of the SS and Gestapo. Did they stay in a hotel or in quarters allocated by the Italians? They couldn't have gone to the hunting hut on Krenbichel; the way there led straight through the partisans' territory.

Documented only by these two snapshots, everything about this trip, its timing and purpose, seems mysterious and bizarre. Studying the photographs, I rack my brains over what can have induced my mother to go somewhere in the middle of a guerrilla war – unless my father hid it from her. And that's something else I'd like to know. What did they talk about during the hours their journey there must have taken them? About his job in Münster? Did he tell her about the colleagues he played handball with in his spare time, about the work they did in the office – the transports of Jews, the executions of forced labourers? Did she ask him what he did? Did she want to hear details? Or did she prefer to be left in the dark? Did she suspect what her lover's duties consisted of? Did it worry her?

I don't believe so. She had a gift for putting such things aside, for blanking out unpleasantness and only seeing what she wanted to see. As she often said, she wasn't interested in politics. Politics was something that only men concerned themselves about. In this respect, like children, they weren't to be taken entirely seriously. The persecution of the Jews and the forced labourers, the expulsion of the Slovenes: that was all politics; that was none of her concern.

She probably didn't want to know overmuch about Münster. I cannot remember ever hearing her say the name of that town. But then again, I never suspected she had been in Gottschee (Kočevje), until I found the pictures of the two of them standing in a field, smiling lovingly at one another.

16

In November 1942 my father was transferred to Einsatzgruppe D as chief of a Sonderkommando (Special Commando). Numbering between 400 and 500 men in total, Einsatzgruppe D consisted of a group of staff officers and of Sonderkommandos 10a, 10b, 11a and 12. He was appointed chief of Sonderkommando 11a. The officers were members of the SD, the SS, the Kripo and the Gestapo; the men came from the Gestapo and the Waffen SS. There were also local auxiliaries to draw on: Russians, Ukrainians and later Circassians, Tatars and members of other ethnic groups. With a motor pool of 170 vehicles, the Einsatzgruppen were highly mobile.

At the start of the war against the Soviet Union, Einsatzgruppe D was attached to the 11th German Army, Army Group South, which advanced through Bukovina and Bessarabia towards the Crimea and then on to the Caucasus. From June 1941 to July 1942 the unit was led by Otto Ohlendorf, after which Walter Bierkamp took command. Otto Ohlendorf, a university professor and intellectual who had worked for the Institute of Applied Economic Science in Berlin before joining the SD, listed the duties of the Einsatzgruppen at the Einsatzgruppen Trial before a US military judge in Nuremberg in 1947: 'The Einsatzgruppen had the following assignments: they were responsible for all political security tasks within the operational area of the army units to which they were attached, and within the rear areas, insofar as the latter did not fall under civil administration. In addition they had the task of clearing the conquered areas of Jews, communist officials and agents. The last named task was to be accomplished by the killing of all racially and politically undesirable elements seized who were considered a danger to security.'

In addition to the Jews, the 'comprehensive ethnic cleansing' was intended to include gypsies, the mentally ill, the handicapped, so-called anti-social elements, communist functionaries and, in general, all those the Germans considered 'Asiatic subhumans'. It was a licence for every sort of mass murder. The terms were so broad that even the leaders of the Einsatzgruppen often seemed at a loss. For instance, after the conquest of the Crimea the question arose as to what should happen to the Krymchaks, one of the small Turkic peoples in the region who at some remote point in history had adopted the Jewish faith. The question was referred to Berlin, where it was decided that the Krymchaks were Jews and were to be treated as such; and so the Krymchaks were shot. 'Living space' had to be created so that Germans – from the South Tyrol, for instance – could settle in the Crimea. Heinrich Himmler, who was responsible for settlement matters, dreamt of turning the Crimea into a Gothic province for his loyal SS.

Concerned about my development, my grandmother always gave me 'good German books' for Christmas. One of these was a four-volume edition of Felix Dahn's *A Fight for Rome*, appropriately enough printed in German, or Gothic, script. I was twelve at the time and thrilled by the tragic story of Totila, the last king of the Goths, and his heroic struggle to prevent the Byzantine generals of Justinian from reconquering Italy.

Otto Ohlendorf said in his statement at Nuremberg that any member of an Einsatzgruppe who had refused an order to take part in a liquidation operation would have been shot – he would have seen to it personally. I presume this was a lie to cover his subordinates, since there are enough reports of high-ranking officials refusing to order their men to shoot or even requesting to be transferred away from an Einsatzgruppe and having their request granted. 'One could at least try,' explained Franz Alfred Six, one of the young intellectuals in SD Main Office in Berlin, after the war. 'In any event no one was shot for it.'

Between June 1941 and July 1943 the Sonderkommandos of Einsatzgruppe D murdered over 90,000 people in southern Russia, mainly Jews. As a rule the victims were shot. They were made to stand on the edge of a pit and shot in the neck or the back of the head so that they fell forwards. Then the next group was lined up and shot, until the pit was full. Sometimes the victims were forced to get into the pit and were shot already lying down. The people behind then had to lie on top of them; some were only badly wounded and were buried alive. From December 1941 Einsatzgruppe D also used gas vans for killing: a 1.5 tonne Opel Blitz, a Saurer and a Deutz truck. The vans had a black metal body and held up to thirty people; they were primarily intended for killing women and children. A hose fed the exhaust fumes back into the van, and the victims died within ten to fifteen minutes. The Russian auxiliaries called the gas vans *Ubitsa duchy*, 'soul killers'.

'The Jews went into the soul killer without a struggle. One didn't need to use any force on them. The explanation for this is probably that these people had frequently seen the soul killer in the courtyard,' a Russian who worked with Einsatzgruppe D testified before a Soviet court after the war. 'They cleaned the van when it came back and so they knew that death awaited them in the soul killer.'

There were officers, however, who refused to use gas vans. One of them was Dr Werner Braune, the head of Sonderkommando 11b of Einsatzgruppe D. At the Einsatzgruppen Trial in 1947, Braune explained that he dispensed with the gas vans because, to his mind, 'execution by shooting was more honourable for both parties'.

138

Like most Sonderkommando chiefs, Werner Braune was a lawyer. He had joined the NSDAP in 1931, the same year as my father. In 1934 Braune was accepted into the SS and the SD simultaneously. In 1938 he was deputy chief of the Gestapo in Münster, and from there he was transferred to Coblenz Gestapo. His and my father's paths crossed time and again: Münster, Coblenz, the RSHA in Berlin, southern Russia.

When the German troops advanced into the Caucasus in the summer of 1942, Sonderkommandos 11a and 11b followed at their heels. They found a population traditionally opposed to Russians and communists, and volunteers flocked to join their ranks. But the Caucasus also had a Jewish population, known as the Mountain Jews, who dressed and lived no differently to the other ethnic groups. Einsatzgruppe D carried out its first major operation in August 1942 in Krasnodar and Ejsk, where it murdered the inmates of mental institutions and children's homes. On 1 September 1942 500 Jews were shot in Mineralnyje Wody. A few days later the Jews of Jessentuki and Kislovodsk were marched to Mineralnyje Wody and shot. Around 10,000 Jews in all were murdered by the Sonderkommandos in the Caucasus.

At the start of December 1942 my father arrived in the Caucasus to take command of Sonderkommando 11a's hundred or so men. He wore the standard field-grey Waffen SS uniform worn by all members of the Einsatzgruppen, with field cap, breeches and top boots, and an SD arm badge on his left forearm. I haven't been able to find out anything about what he did in the Caucasus: no mention in the literature, no documents, no witness testimony, nor any photographs. It is as if he went into a dark tunnel and only came out two months later and no one saw what he had done in there. But I can form a rough idea of what happened in the tunnel.

I remember a day in the Ludwigsburg archives in Baden-Württemberg, a branch of the German National Archives that contains the records of the Central Office of the State Justice Administration for the Investigation of National Socialist Crimes. On the desk in front of me lay a couple of thick files that I had been reading. They were trial transcripts labelled:

Accused: Bierkamp, Walter, *et al.* Unit: Einsatzgruppe D. Country Where Crime Committed: Southern Russia.

I looked out of the window at a tree whose branches almost touched the glass. A short-toed, brown-and-white-speckled treecreeper scurried over the trunk, poking its long, slightly curved beak into the crevices, looking for insects. It was a July day and the sky was cloudless. For two days I had sifted through the material collected in the files: witness testimonies, accounts of executions and the use of gas vans, the 'soul killers'. The activities of Sonderkommando 11a were well documented, including those of its chief, Paul Zapp, who had ordered the shooting of 5,000 Jews in Cherson. Before joining the SD, Paul Zapp had been active in the youth organization of the Protestant Bible Circle Movement and, later, the 'neopagan' German Faith Movement. He had commanded Sonderkommando 11a from the start of the Russian campaign to July 1942, when he was transferred back to Germany (he was arrested in 1967 and sentenced to life imprisonment on 13,449 counts of murder).

But the only piece of information I found concerning the time my father was chief of the Sonderkommando was a memo to the effect that Lieutenant Colonel and Senior Government Counsellor, *Oberregierungsrat,* Dr Gerhard Bast had commanded Sk 11a from November 1942 to December 1942. The rank and professional title are wrong: he was a major and Government Counsellor, *Regierungsrat.* Otherwise I found no trace of him. He had vanished into the tunnel. In a monumental work by the historian Andrej Angrick about the activities of Einsatzgruppe D in the southern Soviet Union from 1941 to 1943, I didn't even find my father's name in the index. I did though find a reference to an SS plan to employ SS skiers in the Caucasus mountains. Perhaps he was sent there as part of that project. Skiing on the Elbrus, long tours which no one had ever done before – what temptation for a passionate mountaineer! But he wasn't to get an opportunity to climb the Elbrus or Kazbek mountains. Militarily the Caucasus adventure was a fiasco. At the start of 1943 the Germans retreated from the Caucasus under mounting pressure from the Red Army. Einsatzgruppe D was disbanded and part of it sent to Belarus, under the name of the 'Bierkamp Combat Group', to combat partisans in the Pripet Marshes.

When I closed the last file, I remember feeling a momentary sense of frustration and disappointment. My eyes stung from reading the old and faded documents, and I hadn't found anything concerning my father. Then I realized what this meant: that the alternative would have been to find a report from the Caucasus signed by my father using phrases like 'the commando's sphere of operations has been rendered *judenfrei*', 'the territory has been mopped up', 'we have combed the area', 'all dangerous elements have been neutralized'. At least this way I could cling to the hope that his time had been spent overseeing his Sonder-kommando's withdrawal from the front line.

I wondered whether I should continue the search in other archives; perhaps I'd come up with some more information there. The Ludwigsburg archivist, a cheerful young man who had prepared the documents for me and answered all my questions very expertly, shook his head. Of course, it wasn't out of the question that I'd discover something new, but it would certainly be difficult. The source situation, as archivists call it, was poor. A lot of material hadn't been worked through; it was scattered between different provinces, and no one could say how much was still in Russian archives. The thought of spending weeks at a time in archives discouraged me. And finding out more wouldn't change anything. I knew enough as it was.

Otto Ohlendorf was sentenced to death at the Einsatzgruppen Trial before the United States Military Tribunal in Nuremberg and hanged. The same fate befell Werner Braune. Walter Bierkamp had committed suicide in April 1945. Erwin Schulz, who had set up the Graz Gestapo in 1938 and employed my father, was also convicted at the Einsatzgruppen Trial. Schulz had been in charge of Sonderkommando 5 of Einsatzgruppe C, which had rampaged through Brody, Berditchev and Lvov. He was sentenced to twenty years' imprisonment. Schulz had made no secret at the time of his objection to the mass shootings and as a result had requested to be relieved of his command. He was transferred back to Berlin, to Reich Security Main Office, there to pursue his career unhindered.

17

When I was ten I had three friends whom I simply thought of as Russian, although they may in fact have been Belorussian: those sorts of distinction weren't important to me then. Oddly enough they were all called Alexander: Alexander Mokotov, Alexander Poscharov, known as Poschar, and Alexander Lebedev, who for some reason was called Schklar. This was in 1954 at the boarding school I attended after elementary school. The school was in Salzburg province, in an isolated valley in the Hohe Tauern seven kilometres from the nearest population centre, Mittersill, a market town in the district of Pinzgau.

The three Russians were the sons of DPs, Displaced Persons, as they were clumsily termed in bureaucratic parlance. Their fathers had presumably served with the Germans and joined the retreat with their families in order finally to end up in Salzburg, where there was a large DPs camp in a part of town called Parsch. Salzburg town and province were in the American zone, and the Americans did not turn over any Russians who had fought with the Germans against the Red Army to the Soviet Union, as the British did the Cossacks. What the fathers of my three friends had done in the war and why they had fled their homeland didn't interest me as a child, and later, when I was old enough to ask, the Russians had gone. They had emigrated with their parents to the USA or Canada or Australia. The Parsch camp had merely been a way station in the turmoil of their lives.

The school, which was often just called Felbertal after the valley it stood in, had other Russian, Yugoslav, Hungarian, Ukrainian and Bulgarian pupils who had come to Austria for similar reasons, as fugitives from what had become communist eastern Europe. But Mokotov, Poschar and Schklar were my immediate neighbours. We stayed in a half-finished building that later housed the joinery and locksmith workshops (we learned a trade at the school and took the master craftsman's qualifying examination alongside the *Matura*). The entire first year – eleven boys in all – slept in a room containing the veneer press.

The boarding school had been founded by a Russian. His grandfather was said to have been master of ceremonies at the Tsars' court, which was presumably one reason why so many Russian refugees' children attended the school. Another was that it was a private school, which in the early days was in dire financial straits. A Protestant organization used to make donations of blankets, crockery and even food. I can still taste the insipid sweetness of the beet jam on my tongue and the sharp tang of the yellow American cheeses (which, from the look of them, must have come ashore with the first GIs in Normandy) that were kept in the room off the kitchen in big round wooden boxes. In exchange for these provisions without an expiry date the school had to agree to take refugees' children.

The olive-green, lined jackets that were sold in the school came from army stores as well. They were second-hand and dirt cheap and, for a while, when every other boy was running around in one, US army jackets were practically the school uniform. An unbelievably shabby uniform, but that only made it all the more appealing to us. In summer, as a personal touch, for years I wore a pair of black velvet corduroy Hitler Youth shorts, which I had inherited from an acquaintance in Amstetten. I loved the HY shorts, not because they were Hitler Youth but because they had lots of handy pockets.

At the start the school was genuinely poor. It didn't even have proper beds. Everything was improvised: the classrooms, the dormitories, the bathrooms. I don't think we had hot water in my first year; at any rate I didn't wash often, which didn't seem to bother anybody. The Russians were older than us, fifteen or sixteen already; from the perspective of a ten-year-old, as I then was, they seemed almost grown-up. I remember admiring them enormously. They were my great role models. They could box, throw knives, build fires, among a multitude of other accomplishments that seemed hugely important to a ten-year-old. Mokotov, beefy and dark-haired, tried to teach me to box. I don't know where he got the boxing gloves from; perhaps he brought them with him from the camp. He was very careful and took great pains not to hurt me. One of them – I think it was Poschar – cut my hair once, to my mother's horror. He was not a gifted barber. Schklar, a gangling, lanky, perpetually cheerful boy, taught me how to throw a knife, at which he was a master. He could fling his knife across an entire room and bury it quivering in a bull's eye painted on the door, but his coaching wasn't a success with me; I never showed much aptitude. Knife throwing was all the rage when I was at the school. Whoever had a suitable knife (virtually everybody, and the bigger the better) practised constantly, and because most of the buildings (huts, an old log cabin called the shooting lodge) were wooden there was no shortage of targets, although you always had to watch out for an unsuspecting individual walking into your line of fire just when you were about to release the knife. Understandably the school caretaker was not an admirer of our virtuosity or the damage we did to the furnishings that had been so painstakingly acquired. It seems a miracle that nobody lost his life, or at least an eye, to a knife during that time.

We were given a lot of freedom at Felbertal. At the beginning it was run on strictly democratic principles that would be inconceivable for a school today. Almost everything was settled by the school council, on which pupils and teachers had equal voting rights. All questions concerning the students were debated endlessly before being put to the vote. These ranged from the food (porridge for breakfast or bread with a tiny bit of butter – initially salted butter from American army surplus stocks), to new pupils and even new teachers – both had to put themselves to a vote by the school council after a probation period. I don't know whether there was ever a vote on the Russians; they were already there when I got to Felbertal, but they didn't actually attend the secondary school (they lacked the necessary qualifications), receiving an elementary-school education instead. I don't even know where they were taught. The different classes were scattered all over the grounds so that it was easy to lose track, and, in any case, the lessons were rather secondary; at least we never talked to the Russians about them – they had more important things to teach us.

Getting to know and even become friends with these Russians early in my life influenced my later development – in my earlier memories of the occupying Soviet soldiers in Amstetten, they always remained exotic strangers and I never had any real contact with them. It marked the beginning of this curiosity for everything to do with the east (perhaps there was a protest against my grandparents in this as well, but it wasn't decisive), a curiosity that ended up determining the course of my studies: Slavonic languages and Eastern European History.

I also have the school to thank for immunizing me against certain influences from my family at an early age. After all, I spent most of nine formative years in Felbertal rather than Linz or Amstetten. Our teachers were very young and inoculated us with something that, if one were to use grand words, one would call tolerance and a democratic attitude. At any rate, no one tried to create links with that image of the past that was revered at home (especially in Amstetten).

My grandmother said she didn't understand where my love of the Slavs had come from when I told her I was going to do Slavonic studies. We were in the Todt inn in Rathausstrasse in

Amstetten, she with a bowl of clear broth in front of her, which she would send back at any moment, and I with a big schnitzel. She didn't say anything about my father having been in Russia, Poland and Slovakia during the war. I only found that out much later. At first she thought of my studies as a whim, which she certainly did not want to endorse, but I was the adored grandson, the beloved son's only child who could get away with a great deal. My uncle, my father's younger brother, simply shook his head. He said that he would never have let me get away with it, but no one had asked him. It wasn't long before the Slavs came between my grandmother and me. She became increasingly impatient when I talked about my studies and my friends in Warsaw. I responded angrily and provoked her with slogans from the student movement that burst onto the scene in 1968. She was hurt, which, with my youthful lack of consideration, I did nothing to remedy, and we grew ever more estranged from one another.

I went to Amstetten less and less, pleading the studies that my grandmother paid for. The definitive break with her and my uncle came about almost incidentally. After I had come back from two years studying in Poland, my grandmother in her helplessness wrote me a letter in which she expressed the (not entirely unfounded) anxiety that one day I might appear in Amstetten with a Polish wife. She wrote that she had to warn me that she could never approve of such a union. The thought that I might marry a Jewish woman was even worse. I must promise her, in remembrance of my father, that I would never do that. She categorically forbade it, otherwise it would be impossible for her to see me. I was twenty-four at the time, a left-wing radical (I considered myself a Trotskyite), probably immature and in any case very self-righteous. Taking myself extremely seriously, I responded with a pompous, implacable letter breaking off relations with my grandmother. I wrote that I didn't want to have anything more to do with her or her family or Amstetten in any shape or form; it was over for good between us and from now on she was to leave me in peace. It was that simple for me. The breach may well have been inevitable, but when I think of that letter today I feel sorrow and shame.

I didn't see my grandmother again, nor did we ever write to each other. We both maintained a grim silence, which must have been far easier for me than for her. When she was dying she said she wanted to see me. My uncle sent a telegram; I left for Amstetten immediately but she died shortly before I arrived. I remember the words my uncle greeted me with at the gate: 'She died like a German woman.'

18

By January 1943 my father was back from the Caucasus. He was not assigned to anti-partisan operations in the Pripet Marshes, like many other members of Einsatzgruppe D, but sent to Linz as chief of the local Gestapo. On 2 February he notified SS Personnel Office at 8 Prinz-Albrecht Strasse in Berlin, 'For official reasons I have been transferred to the Linz (Danube) State Police Office on 25.1.1943. My address is 13 Langgasse, Linz, Danube.'

Thirteen Langgasse was the headquarters of the Linz Gestapo in the former Catholic Young Working Men's hostel. He was allocated a flat in the building. He also began working in the Linz Subordinate Regional HQ of the SD, which occupied the comfortable villa on the Gugl not far from my mother's house. The year before they had gone to Gottschee together for a few days, presumably in secret. Now that he was in Linz, they had plenty of opportunities to meet. I wonder whether she told her husband about the other man, or if he suspected something, if he noticed some change in her behaviour. Perhaps she had been thinking all along of leaving her husband, who was twenty-one years older than her, for my father.

The documents I have been able to find leave it unclear as to why my father was only on active service in the east for two months. Perhaps he got himself transferred back to Linz to be near my mother. Did he have the necessary connections to engineer something like that? In February 1943 Himmler appointed an old acquaintance of my father's to succeed Reinhard Heydrich as head of the Security Police and SD: Dr Ernst Kaltenbrunner, born in Linz, member of a Graz duelling fraternity, leader of the

outlawed Austrian SS, fellow internee of my grandfather in Kaisersteinbruch in 1934. One of the most powerful of all SS men, he might have pulled the necessary strings as a favour for a colleague from Graz and the Ostmark. But this is speculation. What is certain is that my father began working in Linz at the end of January 1943.

When he arrived in the Upper Danube, the public's morale was extremely low, as it was everywhere in the Ostmark. On 3 February a radio newsflash announced the fall of Stalingrad. Many Austrians had fought and died or been taken prisoner there. In a report on the public mood compiled by the Linz SD, the fall of Stalingrad was said to have caused the 'deepest sadness and, in some cases, dejection and despondency' in the Upper Danube. The SD reported calls for an end to the war and even incitements to commit violence against NSDAP officials. When a local party leader had informed a farmer's wife in Grieskirchen of her son's 'hero's death' in the east, she had boxed his ears and cursed him, saying, 'You're to blame for it having come to this.'

War weariness, listlessness and apathy were increasingly apparent among the population, to which the Gestapo responded with ever more severe repression. There was a sharp rise in arrests for offences under the Treachery Law, especially subversion and listening to banned broadcasts from the BBC.

On 26 March 1943 the Linz Gestapo sent a file on a protectorate citizen, Thomas Kotek, to the senior public prosecutor at Linz regional court, 'with a request for an assessment as to prosecution'. My father had signed the letter.

Thomas Kotek was a Czech railway worker on the Bohemian-Moravian Railway who was alleged to have deliberately opened a wagon full of ballast so that the contents spilled over the tracks and blocked them. It had taken the train's escort around ninety minutes to get them clear again. Kotek denied the charge under questioning, but was still sentenced to two years in prison for endangering the work of 'a firm essential to the defence of the Reich'.

On 17 May 1943 my father sent a file to the public prosecutor's office at Linz special court, this time concerning a certain Franz Marchhart, the manager of a farm in Mühlviertel and the father of two children. Someone had informed upon Marchhart and two fellow farm workers, French prisoners of war, accusing them of listening to a BBC broadcast. The farm foreman was given a year and a half in jail for deliberately listening to foreign radio stations' news bulletins and illegally associating with prisoners of war.

Two files of many. The Gestapo even noted mounting insubordination among foreign workers, forced labourers and prisoners of war. 'Breaches of employment contracts' were on the rise. Forced labourers and prisoners of war obviously did not have employment contracts, but that did not prevent them breaching them and thereby incurring draconian penalties. At the end of January 1943 Linz Gestapo office issued an ordinance ruling that henceforth breaches of employment contracts by foreign workers were to be punished exclusively by the Gestapo. Another directive contained the reminder that it was unlawful to ill-treat 'Eastern workers and Poles for work-related offences'. The Gestapo abrogated this right to itself.

'Eastern workers' are those workers of non-German nationality who have been seized in either the Reich Commissariat of the Ukraine, the General Commissariat of White Ruthenia or in areas east of these territories, bordering on the Free States of Latvia and Estonia, and, after occupation by the German Wehrmacht, brought to the German Reich, which is to be understood to include the Protectorate of Bohemia and Moravia, and put to work here. Ukrainians who fall under the above named category of persons are therefore to be designated 'Eastern Workers'. The term 'Russian' is inadmissible.

Everything was regulated by the Gestapo, even down to the question of how foreign workers were to address people: 'With the exception of the Poles, foreign workers cannot be prohibited from using the German greeting *Heil*,' one ordinance read. And every Gestapo directive crossed my father's desk; he had his work cut out for him. In the spring of 1943 the Gestapo set up a 'Labour Education Camp' for foreign 'shirkers' and 'absconders' under its direct control in a Reich Railway stockyard. The notorious Mauthausen concentration camp and adjoining Gusen sub-camp were very close to Linz; the Gestapo ran their own departments in each.

In 1943 the Secret State Police also went after the few Jews who had survived in the Upper Danube in so-called 'protected marriages'. If the Aryan partner died, the Gestapo took immediate action, as, for example, in the case of Alois Smolka, a lawyer from Wels who was arrested for 'friendly contact with individuals of German blood' in August 1943 and imprisoned in Linz. In October 1943 he was deported to Auschwitz, where he died.

Besides his official duties, my father had to command attention, in his well-cut grey uniform with its black collar patch and cap with the black band and death's-head badge with two crossed bones. He had to attend official and social functions, be an ambassador of his office, of the Secret State Police and Security Service of the SS. He was a powerful man, before whom many people humbled themselves.

On 28 March 1943 the Japanese Ambassador in Berlin, Hiroshi Oshima, visited the *Gauhauptstadt* Linz to celebrate the opening of the Linz branch of the German-Japanese Society. Oshima was a personal friend of Hitler's and a fervent believer in National Socialism. His enthusiasm for Nazi Germany earned him the

nickname 'Germany's Ambassador to Germany'. I have a dozen snapshots of this important visit, some hopelessly underexposed, showing the exotic guest during his stay in Linz: Oshima in the Regional Theatre in a box next to the Gauleiter August Eingruber, a thickset man who looks like a butcher; Oshima in front of Linz Castle, at the head of a pack of important men, uniformed and plain-clothed; Oshima outside Leonding cemetery, where Hitler's parents are buried; and, lastly, Oshima bent over the plans for the grandiose rebuilding of Linz, some of which Hitler had drawn himself. My father is in several of the pictures himself, either in uniform or civilian clothes, mainly in the background – but still a part of it all, an attentive observer.

In Linz he at last had the opportunity to go skiing and mountain climbing again, which he had been denied in the Caucasus. From 26 February to 1 March he went on a tour of the Tote Gebirge, staying in the Linzerhaus and the Steirersee hut with colleagues from the Gestapo. 'With *KK* Hurnaus, *KOA* Neumüller, *KS* Pointner, *KS* Scharinger,' he noted in his journal. All these official abbreviations; rank still applied in the mountains. KK stands for criminal commissar, KS for criminal secretary, but what is KOA? *Kriminaloberassistent* (Criminal Senior Assistant)? Some abbreviations, self-evident at the time, are barely decipherable now. This was the forgotten secret code of the terror. 'Fine weather, good snow. Foot giving trouble,' he concludes his journal entry on the trip. Perhaps he had been wounded in the Caucasus; there is no way of knowing.

On 4 April Hitler made a public appearance in Linz, which instantly brought about an improvement in the general mood. If the Führer took the time to visit his home town, the situation at the front couldn't be all that hopeless. The chief of the Linz Gestapo was one of the dignitaries very close to the Führer that day. Did my father enjoy himself that day, I wonder?

19

My mother told me that he had had enough of the Gestapo, that he talked about applying for the colonial service (after winning the war, the official line was that the German Reich would recover at least its former colonies overseas). He had supposedly been promised a governorship or something similar in Africa and had even started to teach himself a native language – she thought she remembered that it was Swahili. I doubt he had a particular gift for languages. As early as 1940 a notice appeared in the Orders of the chief of the Security Police and SD declaring that members of the Security Police and SD could apply for posting to the future German colonies, but it expressly stated that 'prior study of a native language' was not necessary. It is impossible to tell whether my father really put himself forward for training for the future colonial service or whether his alleged wish to get out of the Gestapo was merely a legend that was invented after the war for my sake.

Even during his time in Linz, when he was chief of the Gestapo, my father remains a stereotypical figure to me, confined to a few photographs and documents. Here most of all, in fact, because Linz was my stepfather's town. He was the father I grew up with and called 'Papa' even long after I knew he was not my natural father. We never talked about this, nor was it even so much as intimated. There were many things that weren't talked about; appearances had to be maintained: the appearance of normality, of order, of bourgeois stability, not only outwardly but also within the family. Our relationship was never very intimate or emotional. I always felt a certain distance between us, but I suppose that partly reflected his character – he tended to taciturnity and there was always something of the outsider about him – as well, perhaps, as the age difference between us. He could have been my grandfather.

He had worked in management for a bank until 1942 and then retired to devote himself wholly to painting, which had been his real passion since he was a boy. He often drew the children – my sister, brother and me – and we had to 'sit' for him, as he called it, every year. I sometimes tried to get out of it, because I hated keeping still, but he insisted. I still have all the portraits he did of me, from when I was one year old to when I was a teenager, a coloured chalk drawing for every year; only the first one, in 1945, is black and white, since coloured chalks were not available then. I haven't put up any of the pictures; I keep them in a portfolio. We had to sit for him in his studio in the basement of our house, where he kept one of his few extravagances, a black grand piano, which was a present he had given himself in his old age.

He played it only rarely, 'improvising' he called it (to his regret he had never taken piano lessons). Otherwise he was tremendously modest, ascetic almost, in what he ate, how he dressed and all other material matters. I still remember dropping in on them once unexpectedly and finding him on his own. My mother was away and even Resi, who was nominally our daily but in reality much more than that – nanny, aunt, older friend to the children – wasn't there for some reason. He was very impractical when it came to everyday life, such as cooking, for example; he couldn't even scramble an egg. The two women had filled the fridge from top to bottom with apple strudel, which he liked. He ate apple strudel morning, noon and night for a week, or even longer, and was perfectly content. When I offered to buy some food for us both, he asked in amazement, 'What for? What about the apple strudel?' He had only eaten half; there was still so much left.

We had a large vegetable garden and plenty of fruit trees, which yielded crops in summer and autumn that would have provided for several large families. He would often come into the kitchen in the morning, when Resi was already at work, with a pail filled to the brim with fallen apples that were starting to go bad, and timidly ask the patently rhetorical question: could one ('one', not 'she', as if there might have been any other candidate for the job) turn the windfall to use? He derived particular satisfaction from the phrase 'turn to use', like all of his generation who had lived through two wars and all they entailed – food shortages, rationing, devastation of cities, loss of homes – and so knew how important it was to salvage everything that in some way could be turned to use. The verb 'to throw away' did not exist in his vocabulary. Everything was kept: perhaps some purpose could be found for it. Apples and pears were carefully laid out on shelves in the cellar, no two pieces of fruit touching. On another shelf next to the apples he kept things he had found while gardening: bomb splinters, bits of rusty iron, other junk – one never knew. He maintained this ethos of extreme thriftiness even in times of relative prosperity, and my mother was the only exception to its iron principle: if he had been able, he would have showered her with presents.

'If the master'll put it there,' Resi would say, sighing, with a look at the pail, and immediately set to work peeling the apples for apple strudel, apple turnover, apple purée or apple jelly. She had an extensive repertoire of delicacies she could conjure up from the windfall, otherwise bound for the compost heap. When speaking to my mother and stepfather, Resi used the third person of domestic servants and well-brought up children which even then belonged to a bygone age.

My stepfather's love of gardening has been passed on to me. I love digging in the soil, sowing lettuces, planting trees, and I am somebody who picks up everything they find as well: it's all collected – rusty iron, animal bones, interesting-looking stones – nothing is ever thrown away. Sometimes I catch myself talking to myself as I show him some lettuces that I'm proud of. He died in 1968.

Looking back, I realize that we never once had an open conversation that even touched upon my birth and my family in Amstetten, or his position as honorary head of the Reich Chamber for Fine Arts in Upper Danube, or even my natural father's job as chief of the Linz Gestapo. He must have known my father, but he never made any disparaging comments about him. He said nothing about any of these subjects, and I didn't ask. A profound muteness prevailed between us, which for a long time seemed perfectly normal to me.

20

In the summer of 1943 my father went climbing again, mainly in the Styrian mountains – the Ennstal Alps, the Gesäuse – that he had known since childhood. I don't think my mother ever went with him; his journal is full of names, but hers is not one of them. They presumably met up in Linz and the Salzkammergut, by the Traunsee, or in Gmunden or Bad Ischl. A photograph shows my father on a lake, perhaps the Traunsee; he is rowing a flat-bottomed skiff. On the right of the picture there is a strip of shore, a wooded slope falling to the water, and a few boathouses and landing stages. Perhaps my mother went out onto one of the landing stages to take a picture of him as a souvenir. *A wonderful day at the Traunsee.* I wonder how she explained her absence at home. Did she tell her husband, my stepfather, the plain truth? Did their acquaintances whisper and make remarks? Linz wasn't a big town and it can hardly have been possible to keep an affair secret for long, especially one with the chief of the local Gestapo.

He had to be careful too. The SS set considerable store, at least outwardly, on its members being beyond reproach. If an SS man began a relationship with the wife of a party comrade, he could get into trouble. The SS had to be not just a 'racial' but also an 'ethical' élite. A German knightly order. Moreover, Himmler required that where possible the members of his order start a family between the ages of twenty-five and thirty. My father was already thirty-two in 1943. He had obtained various SS decorations during his career, the silver death's-head ring and the Yule candleholder (members of the SS were given this so that they

could celebrate the Yule festival with due solemnity). He had also joined the Lebensborn, the 'Fount of Life' Association, although that was compulsory for all full-time SS men and membership dues were automatically deducted from their wages. But it is clear from his file that he never received the Honour Sword of the Reichsführer of the SS, which was personally awarded by Himmler.

The SS's pseudo-Teutonic paraphernalia and institutions – the runic double S, the Yule candleholder, the death's-head rings, the Order Castles,* the Lebensborn breeding programme – were all designed to emphasize the SS's élite position in the party. Legally this was reflected in the special jurisdiction all members of the SS, the SD and the Security Police enjoyed in the German Reich and the occupied territories. The SS and Security Police had separate

*Institutions at Krössinsee, Vogelsang and Sonthofen to train future genera-
tions of SS, based on an amalgam of the Knights Templar and the Order of
Teutonic Knights in East Prussia in the thirteenth century.

courts which were exempted from normal jurisdiction and essentially followed military criminal law.

On 31 May 1944 the SS and Police Court VII in Vienna sentenced SS Major and Government Counsellor Dr Gerhard Bast, chief of the Linz Gestapo, to four months' imprisonment for manslaughter.

The penal order of the court, which was sent to the accused and which I found in my father's papers, stated: 'You are charged with having caused a person's death through culpable negligence in Spilberg on 14.11.1943, in that, while unloading your sporting gun, you handled it with such lack of care that the gun went off and mortally wounded a beater.'

On the day in question SS notables had organized a shoot in the Donau water meadows between the ruined Spilberg Castle and Gusen concentration camp, and my father had gone along, accompanied by Franz Ziereis, the commandant of Mauthausen and its sub-camp Gusen, and Josef Plakolm, the Linz Chief of Police. One of the beaters was a twelve-year-old boy, Alois Klaubauf, from the nearby town of Langenstein. A forester called Missbauer assigned each beater their patch of ground. After the first drive the beaters were called off and went to join the hunters, who were gathered on an avenue that goes through the water meadows. There a shot was fired and Alois Klaubauf collapsed; one of the hunters was a doctor, but he could only confirm that the boy was dead and had been shot in the heart.

The different accounts I have read of the accident all broadly agree. The SS trial papers say that Bast had been about to unload his shotgun and was pointing the barrel at the ground when two shots were fired behind him. He had instinctively turned so that the barrel was pointing upwards and then, as he tried to cock the gun, the hammer, 'probably because of the cool, damp weather', had slipped from under his thumb. An eyewitness and friend of the dead boy, who later wrote a local history of Langenstein with a page devoted to 'the senseless death of Alois Klaubauf', concurred with the verdict of culpable negligence which, since the marksman was holding the barrel level, pointing at the beater, had ended in tragedy.

A shooting accident. A chain of unfortunate circumstances with fatal consequences. When I think about Alois Klaubauf, who was shot in the avenue close to Gusen concentration camp because my father ignored a basic rule of shooting and kept his gun level rather than pointing upwards, the photo of the three-year-old in the smock and apron comes into my mind, clasping a rifle as big as himself in his child's hand; his proud expression, his chin proudly thrust out towards the photographer – 'Look, a real rifle! My first rifle!' That was in 1914 in Laibach (Ljubljana). The spell cast by guns, the bluish shimmer of the steel barrel on which every impress of a finger leaves marks that have to be carefully cleaned off with a soft cloth; nothing must sully the pristine steel.

At the place where it happened in the Gusen water meadow – still in the shadow of the concentration camp today – a memorial stone was erected after the war, an undressed block of granite (presumably from the Dirnberger quarry in Langenstein municipality where Gusen's prisoners slaved and died) with an iron cross rising from it and a figure of Christ crucified. Carved in the stone are the words 'In Memory of 1943'.

My father was sentenced to four months in prison for the manslaughter of the twelve-year-old beater Alois Klaubauf. A week before his sentencing, I was born in Linz Gynaecological Hospital, which had been moved to Bad Hall at the end of 1943 because the bombing of Linz itself was becoming increasingly severe. In the SS trial records, it says that the convicted man is chief of the Linz Gestapo office, '33 years old, single (wants to marry shortly)'. He must have already applied to the relevant SS authorities, the RSHA in Berlin, for a marriage permit. Had he revealed that his prospective bride was already married and was shortly to give birth to his child? Either way, the shooting accident and subsequent sentence put paid to any marriage plans for the time being.

My father didn't go to prison. The highest judicial authority, SS Obergruppenführer and Police General Ernst Rudolf Querner, a passionate hunter himself, ruled that the sentence should be suspended on probation to give the convicted man an opportunity to serve in the east. The decision was submitted to Heinrich Himmler for approval, who said he agreed with the suspension of the sentence but ordered that 'Dr Bast be transferred away from Linz and employed in the east immediately'.

The Reichsführer of the SS made no allowances for personal misconduct on the part of his subordinates. He expected his men to murder the innocent and unarmed without batting an eyelid: Jews, gypsies, the mentally ill, communist officials, Poles, Czechs, Slovenes, women and children. But when one of them caused the death of a fellow German in a fatal shooting accident, that was severely punished. One sort of killing was not equivalent to another. Mass murder was a duty; involuntary manslaughter was a sign of failure. And failure was not tolerated in the SS.

The shooting accident on 14 November 1943 ended my father's career in the Gestapo. But the Nazi bureaucracy worked slowly – the incident had to be reported to Berlin, an investigation opened, witnesses questioned – and in the meantime he remained in his post.

I happened to come across a copy of a letter that he wrote three days after the shooting in the Gusen meadow in his capacity as chief of the Linz Gestapo. The letter is in the Slovenian State Archives in Ljubljana, among papers relating to the Marburg (Maribor in Slovenian) Gestapo. Addressed to the

Marburg an der Drau Branch Office of the Graz Secret State Police, it concerns a Slovenian prisoner called Josef Jersche, born in Tüffer on 4 March 1888, who was a registrar by profession. The abovementioned, the letter runs, was arrested in Marburg in July 1942 on a charge of listening to enemy broadcasts and circulating their news bulletins. He had been in Mauthausen concentration camp since August 1942. My father wrote that he had received a request from Tüffer to look into Jersche's case. It was alleged that Jersche had only been arrested because he had been denounced, and that the informer, a previous mayor of Tüffer, had himself since been arrested for abuse of his position, embezzlement and theft and sentenced to several years in prison.

I request you check whether this information is accurate and, if appropriate, whether a release of Jersche from Mauthausen concentration camp would be justifiable. Jersche is Slovenian but he is reportedly from an old Tüffer family and has always behaved decently. If appropriate, I request you set Jersche's release in motion.

Please inform me of the outcome by return. Dr Bast, Sturmbannführer.

The obvious assumption is that Jersche was an acquaintance of my father's family, which was from the same place. Perhaps Uncle Drolc from Tüffer had interceded on his behalf; perhaps my grandfather from Amstetten had too – he and the registrar were the same generation. The letter casts another light on the chief of the Linz Gestapo who, three days after an event that would destroy his career, took the time to intervene on behalf of a Slovenian prisoner in Mauthausen.

The Marburg Gestapo evidently did not react very promptly to the intervention from Linz, since my father reminded them of it in an express letter stamped 'Very Urgent'.

Re: My letter of 17 November 1943

I call your attention to the abovementioned letter and request your earliest response.

I haven't been able to find out what happened to the prisoner Josef Jersche, but his name, at any rate, is not on the list of those who died in Mauthausen.

Tüffer. Even in wartime, as a senior Gestapo official, my father maintained his links with the little market town in Lower Styria, which had been part of Slovenia since 1918. Emotional ties, which otherwise he only rarely permitted himself, bound him to the place he persistently called by its Slovenian name in the captions to his photographs, where he had spent long summers with his Slovenian Uncle Drolc and his aunt Pauline Bast. There are two other small photographs that refer to the area where he grew up which I find extremely puzzling. They both show a group of cheerful young people out hiking. They are standing or sitting by the side of a gravel road; a few have mountain boots, one has an accordion, they seem to be laughing and enjoying themselves; some are calling something out to the photographer, and my father is in their midst, joining in their laughter, friends with them all. You can't see much of the landscape, just some hills in the background in a blurred haze; perhaps they're part of the Samobor hills. The text on the back baffles me. My father has written 'Samobor 15.IV.1944' and, above that, someone else has written 'Franc'.

In April 1944 my mother was heavily pregnant with his child in Linz, and the SS Court in Vienna had opened an investigation into the shooting accident in Langenstein. And yet this is when he went on a trip to Samobor, a small place in Croatia near the Slovenian border, which was popular with hikers and mountain walkers. I don't know which of the young men in the picture is Franc, but the spelling suggests he was Slovenian. Judging from their looks and dress, all the young men and women could be Slovenian. Perhaps they were from Laško. It is barely 60 kilometres from there to Samobor; they could have gone on a day trip.

In April 1944? With a member of the Gestapo and SS Sturmbannführer, who jokes and laughs with them? It is hard to imagine, but there are the two photographs: 'Samobor 15.IV.1944. Franc.'

21

In June 1944 the Soviet army had launched a major offensive between the Pripet Marshes and the Dvina and forced Army Group Centre to withdraw on a broad front. My father was transferred to BdS Minsk, BdS being *Befehlshaber*, the Commander-in-Chief of the Security Police and SD. He was appointed chief of Sonderkommando 7a of Einsatzgruppe B. By this stage, Minsk was already in Russian hands and the German troops, including Einsatzgruppe B and its five commandos, were in retreat.

When my father set out on the journey east, I cannot say. On 1 July he was still in Amstetten with his parents. A farewell visit. There are two small-format photographs of him alone in his parents' garden, standing under trees whose foliage casts bizarre shadows on the sandy path. It is a sunny day. He is dressed in the field uniform of the Waffen SS, with the cap with the death's head and an SD arm badge on his left forearm. There is a third picture of him with his parents: his father, my grandfather, knock-kneed in *lederhosen* (which was almost a Nazi civilian uniform amongst city-dwelling adults, Hitler being their model) and Styrian jacket, stares indifferently past the photographer as if he had got into the picture by accident. Grandfather had joined the SS shortly before, aged sixty-four; he was given Number 340.111 and the rank of SS Untersturmführer, honorary, which did not entitle him to a uniform. He looks irritable in the photo. Perhaps he couldn't reconcile himself to the fact that his son, for whom he had bought his first rifle, had committed manslaughter and killed a beater. My father and grandmother, on the other hand, are smiling at the camera – my grandmother is beaming, in fact; you can see how

proud she is of her son in uniform. He wears a decoration on his
left breast, the War Service Cross, 2nd Class, with swords, which
he had won in January that year, after the shooting accident. I
have not been able to find any record of what it was that he did in
the Caucasus, but he must have won the medal for something he
was involved in there. War decorations were not awarded for
service in the Linz Gestapo, and the Upper Danube was not yet a
war zone at the start of 1944.

My mother in the meantime was at home with her husband in
Linz. I presume that my father had seen her and his child before
leaving for the east. My mother told me that I was not an attrac-

tive baby, and the few photographs from the time bear her out. I was fat, with a broad nose and a bald head, and, to make matters worse, had contracted jaundice in the clinic in Bad Hall. I was affectionately known as Genghis Khan by the nurses. I found a lock of my hair tied up with a bit of thread between two blank pages of my father's journal, but that must have come later, since I didn't have a hair on my head in July 1944.

By the start of July 1944 Sonderkommando 7a had reached Białystok on the border with Belarus, where, for a short while, it was leaderless. The former chief, SS Sturmbannführer Helmut Looss, was ordered back to Berlin ('After handing over official business to SS Sturmbannführer Dr Bast, you are to report immediately to Office Head 1 in Reich Security Main Office to receive further instructions') and left the unit before his successor had arrived. Besides members of the Gestapo, SD and Kripo, the Sonderkommando included Russian interpreters and volunteers, the so-called *Hiwis* (*Hilfswillige*, Indigenous Volunteers), who wore Waffen SS uniforms without the national eagle or the runes on the collar. There were roughly 180 men in all, divided into various smaller units, which occasionally lost contact with one another in the general chaos of the retreat. On 20 July 1944 the bulk of the commando was in Wygoda, a village north-east of Białystok. Members of the Sonderkommando still remembered the date many years later because it was the day of von Stauffenberg's assassination attempt on Hitler.[*] Wygoda was where my father joined his unit.

What sort of people did he now have under his command? Einsatzgruppen personnel fluctuated a great deal, they were constantly being transferred back and forth, but there was a long-serving core of men who had taken part in the Sonderkommando's

[*]The bomb planted by Colonel Claus Schenk von Stauffenberg which failed to kill Hitler was part of a plot, known as the July Plot, led by senior military leaders such as Field Marshal Erwin von Witzleben and General Ludwig von Beck.

operations in the spring of 1942 under their then chief Albert Rapp. Rapp had ordered numerous mass executions in Russia, including massacres in Klinzy, Dobrush, Starodub and other towns. After the war these shootings were described by a number of eyewitnesses, among them a military policeman who had been with his unit in Klinzy in central Russia in the spring of 1942, on the railway line between Gomel and Brjansk.

The witness, a police officer in civilian life (a profession which he took up again after the war as if nothing had happened) who is called Josef B. in the transcripts, recalled how he had once wanted to see these executions for himself and asked his interpreter to find out when the next big shooting was going to take place. The interpreter (a Russian of German extraction) made enquiries, and together they drove to a wooded area near Klinzy stadium, where the preparations were under way for a so-called 'action'. They came to a long pit about two and a half metres deep and three metres broad, around which members of the SD and the Russian Order Service (OD) were assembled. The victims, Jews and gypsies, were brought to the woods in lorries. The witness remembered that the SD and OD men stood in two rows, forming a corridor from the lorries to the pit along which they drove the victims. At the end were two SD men who positioned the adult victims in front of them, shot them in the back of the head with a pistol and then shoved them into the pit. It was mainly women and children who were shot, some of them mothers with babies; the witness could still picture some of the women giving their children the breast on the way to the pit to calm them down. At the pit the children were torn from their mothers and were generally shot first, in front of their mothers. Josef B. told the investigating judge that very small children were held up by one of their arms by the SD men, shot in the head and then carelessly tossed into the pit like a log. Older children had to lie face down at the edge of the pit. The SD men bent down and shot them in the head from above and then kicked them equally carelessly into the pit. The witness said he could still remember a small boy of no more than ten crying and asking his mother something over and over as they walked towards the pit. He had asked his interpreter what the boy wanted. The interpreter answered that the boy was asking his mother whether it would hurt.

As a rule the shootings were carried out with the service pistol, a PPK 7.65 mm that took six bullets in its magazine. When the magazine was empty, the man stepped back to fit a new one and someone else took his place.

By his own account, the witness watched this procedure for two hours, after which he felt he had seen enough and drove back to his quarters. According to Operation Report No. 194 of 21.4.1942, a total of 1,657 people were shot by Sonderkommando 7a, including 1,558 Jews, forty-five gypsies and twenty-seven partisans and communists. Albert Rapp was considered a 'fierce dog' by his men; they even wrote a song about their commander that was sung to the tune of an old sea shanty, 'We Lay at Anchor off Madagascar'; the first line was 'We fight for Rapp's honour . . .'

The honour of the Germans, an honourable man, conduct that does one honour – how often did I hear such phrases when I was growing up. 'Your father always behaved honourably,' my grandmother impressed upon me. 'If anyone asks you what he did, say he was a government counsellor.'

Albert Rapp considered it vital that every member of the Sonderkommando take part in the shootings; everyone had to prove their 'eastern steadfastness', their hardness. In early 1943 he was wounded in a partisan operation and relieved of his command. (After the war Rapp went into hiding; he was arrested in 1961 and in 1965 sentenced by Essen District Court for 1,180 cases of murder to penal servitude for life.) Thereafter, Sonderkommando 7a was chiefly employed in suppressing the partisans; individual actions were given ingenious code names like 'Frost

Flower' or 'Mudlark'. There were supposedly no mass shootings under the command of Helmut Looss, which does not mean that any Jews in hiding who were captured in anti-partisan sweeps were not liquidated.

When I read the accounts of the massacres, which were described by a range of witnesses as if they were tourist attractions one wouldn't want to miss on holiday,* I wondered whether my father was any different or any better than Albert Rapp and the other Einsatzgruppen chiefs who had ordered the mass shootings. Would he have behaved exactly the same in their place? Does it make a difference whether one gives orders for five or ten or fifty or five hundred people to be shot? Is that just a technical question, a question of logistics?

In July 1944 my father set off towards Warsaw with these men who had taken part in the massacres in Russia (some 'with relish', as one member of the Sonderkommando later remembered), and the front followed close behind. Somewhere on the way to Warsaw – or perhaps beyond it, the testimony differs on this point – the Sonderkommando took between fifteen and twenty Poles hostage. They were apparently landowners, who had been accused of giving the Polish partisans money. On 31 July 1944, the day before the outbreak of the Warsaw Uprising, the commando passed through the capital, which was still quite calm. Sonderkommando 7a, now also known as the 'Bast Sonderkommando' after its new chief, first took up quarters in Błonie, thirty-two kilometres west of Warsaw, and then part of the unit, including the command staff and baggage, was moved to the Radziejowice estate near the textile town of Żyrardów, while the rest stayed in Błonie or were divided up between the surrounding villages. Members of the commando described the Radziejowice

---

*After the war, photo albums belonging to members of the Einsatzgruppen were found to contain pictures of the executions; snapshots that were clearly personal mementoes.

manor house, which belonged to a Countess Krasiński, as a *schloss*, a castle. They remembered a one-storey, brightly painted building with a turret that stood on a small lake, fed by a little stream called the Pisia and surrounded by vegetable gardens and fields. Besides the manor house there were farm buildings, a sawmill and a flour mill. The hostages were locked in a building that an eyewitness described as a sort of citadel. None of the original furnishings of the manor house were left; the meagre furniture came from army stocks. Sonderkommando 7a was stationed in Radziejowice until the middle of September.

It is hard to piece together what my father and his men did during those weeks on the estate. After the war, members of the Sonderkommando testified before a series of examining magistrates that they had sat around doing nothing, played football, gone hunting in the surrounding countryside, fished a little in the tiny river and in general had a good time. As they were enjoying this good time, however, the uprising of the Polish Home Army was raging in Warsaw less than thirty kilometres away; 40,000 people were fighting on either side and the battle lasted until the start of October. On days when there was an east wind, thick black clouds of smoke would have blown over from Warsaw, where the Germans were setting whole rows of houses on fire, one after the other, to smoke out the insurgents and civilians sheltering within them. The rumbling thunder of the guns must have been audible far beyond Radziejowice.

On the Polish side the uprising, which the Germans crushed with every possible means and the greatest possible brutality, claimed 170,000 dead (20,000 fighters and 150,000 civilians), many of whom were victims of mass shootings. The Germans lost around 10,000 men. After the uprising had been put down, the Polish capital, which had already been devastated by the fighting, was reduced to ruins with flame-throwers and dynamite.

It is hard to imagine that the SS and police commanders in

Warsaw, whose men the insurgents had pressed hard at first, would have forgone the services of a unit specialized in liquidating partisans and civilians, especially when it was so close. Some members of the Sonderkommando, including my father, left Radziejowice several times in a car, that much is certain. After the war a witness said that Dr Bast had once gone to Warsaw, supposedly to collect any provisions that he could find lying around; several members of the Sonderkommando accompanied him on that occasion. Another witness, the Sonderkommando's administrative officer, went with him on a number of trips after the start of the uprising. He reported that once they had met a car containing SS Obergruppenführer Erich von dem Bach-Zelewski and several other officers. Bach-Zelewski said that he had been put in charge of suppressing the uprising and he wanted to hold a briefing that evening; he expected Dr Bast to be there. The administrative officer, who could still remember that Bach-Zelewski was drunk when they saw him, said that Bast attended the meeting. But what was discussed, he could not say.

'I don't know about that.' 'I didn't see that.' 'I didn't hear anything about that.' 'I didn't notice that. I wasn't there.' These and similar phrases constantly recur in the witness testimonies gathered during the twenty years after the war. Collective amnesia, blindness, deafness. 'We didn't know anything.'

The crushing of the Warsaw Uprising had no effect on the course of the war. In June 1944 the Allies landed in Normandy, and in the south of France in August. The Soviet troops continued to advance unchecked. They had reached Warsaw during the uprising but stayed on the right bank of the Wiechsel, in the Praga district, without coming to the assistance of the insurgents. In August an uprising also broke out in Slovakia, which at first was directed against the pro-Hitler regime. When the fighting spread, German troops marched into Slovakia, and Sonderkommando 7a was ordered to join them.

In the middle of September the men and all the equipment were entrained at Żyrardów. The hostages who the Sonderkommando had taken to Radziejowice were shot. We know this from a member of Sk 7a who was a driver and secretary in Radziejowice. 'I remember,' he stated, 'that one day in Radcziowicze [*sic*] around twenty Poles were shot.' They were shot in the estate's park. The witness couldn't say who ordered the shooting, Dr Bast or his deputy; all that had stuck in his mind was that the hostages were killed. They couldn't be taken to Slovakia after all – they would have been worthless there – so they were liquidated. That is what the Sonderkommando was there for: to shoot people, Jews, gypsies, Polish hostages. Clearly it didn't occur to anyone to release the Polish landowners before the Sonderkommando left. Whether my father gave the execution order himself (perhaps he was at a meeting with General von dem Bach-Zelewski at the time) is hardly important. He was head of the Sonderkommando that was named after him; he bore responsibility for its actions; the blood of between fifteen and twenty hostages (there's uncertainty about the exact figures; a few more or less dead made no odds) is legally on his hands.

I only found out about the shooting of these hostages – about the Sonderkommando's whole tour of duty in Poland under my father, in fact – while I was working on this book, after I had been involved with Poland for forty years. I studied in Warsaw and I translate Polish literature. It baffled her, my grandmother sometimes used to say, why I was especially interested in Poland, in the Polish language and in Polish literature. She couldn't fathom what had brought me to it. Now I understand the look of incredulity that would come over her face.

22

It was a bitterly cold November morning when I drove out of Banská Bystrica up into the mountains towards Ružomberok. Hoar frost glistened like sugar crystals on the brown grass, bare bushes and rubbish sacks beside the road. Washing hung frozen on a line in one garden, swinging like boards in the wind. On the Velka Fatra, the mountain range between Banská Bystrica and Ružomberok, I was caught in a violent snowstorm that seemed to blow up out of nowhere and then die away equally abruptly. Rožumberok, when I reached it, lay peacefully in the pale winter sunshine.

Six weeks after entering the country, Sonderkommando 7a established its headquarters in this central Slovakian town, known as Rosenberg in German. On leaving Poland in September 1944 my father and his men were first stationed in Senica, a small town north of Bratislava, with a couple of small groups in Myjava and Stará Turá. Their main job was to track down the Slovak partisans, officially called 'bandits' by the Germans. Slovakia's thinly populated mountainous region was an ideal centre for the partisans, who began forming units in 1943 and linked up with Slovak resistance fighters, escaped Soviet prisoners of war and Jews. The Sonderkommando went after any Jews still hiding in the villages or woods of its area with particular fervour (Slovakia's clerical-fascist regime had already organized the deportation of 58,000 Jews to German death camps in 1942). They were either shot on the spot or deported to Sered labour camp, which the Slovak regime had set up for Jews and the Germans turned into a concentration camp, sending a stream of transports from there to Auschwitz.

In Slovakia, Sonderkommando 7a became part of Einsatz-gruppe H (rather than Einsatzgruppe B), which was based in Bratislava and had been specifically formed to crush the uprising. It was commanded by SS Standartenführer (Colonel) Josef Witiska, a close acquaintance of my father from Graz, where they had both worked for the Gestapo. An Operational Situation Report submitted by Sk 7a for the period of 27 September to 7 October 1944 states, under 'II: Jews':

> An action to arrest Jews was carried out in the commando's area of operations between 1.10 and 6.10.1944. In collabora-tion with the Hlinka Guard and the Slovak Gendarmerie, a total of 158 Jews were arrested.

This terse account does not spell out that, once arrested, all the Jews were murdered, but it didn't need to. Named after the priest and nationalist politician Andrej Hlinka, who lived in Rožumberok until his death in 1938, the Hlinka Guard was a paramilitary unit of roughly 5,000, which co-operated closely with the Germans and was known for its anti-Semitic excesses.

On 22 September 1944 my mother sent my father a photo of her with me on her arm standing in front of a clump of bushes (I think I know the spot in our garden in Linz where the picture was taken). I am four months old and have no hair; she is smiling happily. She has written the date on the back; he had been in Slovakia for a week exactly. His address is: Dr Gerhard Bast, Sonderkommando 7a, c/o Chief of Einsatzgruppe H of the Security Police and SD in Pressburg (Bratislava).

So she must have known that he was the head of a Sonder-kommando. I don't know if she had any idea of what a Sonder-kommando's duties consisted of, or if she ever asked him about them. We never talked about it, at any rate.

Nor do I know if he visited us during his time in Slovakia,

from September 1944 to March 1945. Trips back to the *Heimat-kriegsgebiet*, the Home Front, as the Ostmark was already officially called, needed Witiska's express authorization, and besides, my mother was still married to, and living with, my stepfather. In any event there's no mention of a trip of that sort in the few surviving records of Sonderkommando 7a. Much later, when I was about fourteen, my mother gave me a letter – presumably the only one – which he had sent me at the time. It was written in block capitals and decorated with pretty drawings of animals and people in coloured pencil, a little picture book to remind the son, who could not yet read, of his loving father. At some stage I burned the letter in a fit of despair or rage. I don't remember any of the story.

On 30 October the President of the Slovak Republic awarded my father the 3rd Class War Victory Cross with swords 'for outstanding service': it is not hard to guess which sort of service. (He obtained three decorations in all in the just under seven months he spent in Slovakia: the War Victory Cross, the 1st Class Military Service Cross with swords and the silver 2nd Class Eastern

Peoples Service Medal.) At the start of November Sonder-kommando 7a was transferred north-east by train from Senica to Ružomberok, where it was billeted in the District Courthouse. It took over the prison in the same building, the Old Fort as it was known, on the right bank of the River Váh, and set up support points and checkpoints, often only consisting of a few men, in the nearby villages of Turčiansky Martin, Trstená, Liptovský Mikuláš and Námestovo.

As I was looking for the Old Fort on the Váh, I came across an enormous supermarket. At first, from a distance, I thought it actually was a prison, since its façade and part of its roof had been modelled on a penitentiary, and it had watchtowers at every cor-ner like a film set. A little piece of Disneyland. What was left of the fort was immediately behind the supermarket; the stone walls looked newly renovated, but the windows were boarded up. I asked someone working in the supermarket what was going to happen to the old ruin, and he shrugged his shoulders and said that different plans were being discussed.

I went for a walk around the town, starting in the small pedes-trianized zone in the old part in the centre, Podhora, Panská and Mostová Streets. Town houses from the 1870s, crumbling façades, dark gateways, cheaply converted shops with lots of plastic; a mobile-phone shop fitted out all in orange – orange furniture, orange walls, shop assistants in orange jackets – thronged with young people; music blaring from the loudspeak-ers that some of the shops had rigged up on the street. Some gypsies were working on a demolished plot, levelling the build-ing rubble with iron rakes and shovels. A police car drove slowly past, a young policeman coldly inspecting me through the kind of mirrored sunglasses American highway patrolmen wear in Hollywood films. I suddenly found myself in front of the empty synagogue in Panská Street, a tall 1880s building in the Moorish style drowsing in the sun. I saw a few broken windowpanes but none of the anti-Semitic graffiti you find everywhere in Poland. Ružomberok had a Jewish community of approximately 900 before the war, mainly prosperous merchants, doctors and lawyers, of whom only a handful survived the Holocaust. Opposite the synagogue, in front of the cosily named Včela (Bee) café, a group of young men in leather jackets stood smoking and spitting on the ground at regular intervals, as if on cue. A steep set of stairs led up to the church that towered white and commanding over the city, flanked by the mausoleum of Andrej Hlinka, the great shepherd of the nation, the *vel'ky Gazda*. A monument shows a tall, ascetic figure, a Slovakian Savonarola, who nowadays is once more revered as a hero. I returned to the Kultúra Hotel, which shared its premises with the Arts Centre, a sturdy pre-war building that had gained nothing from its renovation, as a postcard in my room showing it next to its 1920s incarnation bore out.

I found a document in the Museum of the Slovak Uprising archives in Banská Bystrica recording a visit of the Slovak Minister of the Interior and chief of the Hlinka Guard, Alexander (Šano) Mach, to Ružomberok on 9 December 1944. He had dinner in the Arts Centre with the Commandant of the German troops stationed in the town and the chief of the SD, SS Sturmbannführer Dr Bast. The Slovak Minister of the Interior and my father agreed that the joint Slovak and German forces must take uncompromising measures against the insurgents and Jews. Both stressed the excellent spirit of collaboration between the Hlinka Guard and the German police.

I sat in the hotel's spacious dining room with a glass of red wine in front of me, the only guest. A chubby young waitress in a miniskirt and white apron stood in a corner, watching me intently. I didn't dare even move my hand, since she took the slightest stirring as an invitation to come running to my table and ask if I wanted anything, which I didn't. I just sat there as if paralyzed and looked out at the street where dusk was slowly gathering.

The Sonderkommando carried out numerous operations against partisans in the Ružomberok area. Often these were so-called 'punitive actions', retaliation for attacks on Germans living in Ružomberok (Rosenberg to them) and the surrounding villages. There was a substantial German minority in central Slovakia and massacres had been committed in several small towns, including Ružomberok, at the start of the uprising. When members of Sonderkommando 7a were tried in German courts after the war, they tended only to want to remember these anti-partisan operations and stressed that their specific roles had been restricted to reconnaissance work and other preparatory duties. They had not taken part in any military actions. Those had been left to the Russian (or Ukrainian, opinions differed) auxiliaries, a company of 'alien' Waffen SS under SS Untersturmführer (Second Lieutenant) Claudius Billerbeck, consequently known as 'Billerbeck Company'. One witness, the owner of a taxicab company, stated in Nuremberg in 1971 that, at all events, no war crimes were committed when he was in the Sonderkommando, nor were any Jews even shot. He said that he always made sure that Jews didn't remain in his sector and that if some were reported, he saw to it that no one learnt their whereabouts. Another witness, Josef Maurer, the Sonder-kommando's motor transport sergeant, said that he had 'not even realized there were any military actions in Slovakia'. The maintenance of the unit's vehicles took up all his time. 'I didn't know anything about partisans or anyone else being shot in Rosenberg,' he testified.

Questioning of František Brettschneider, the Sonder-kommando's interpreter in Ružomberok, in a Czech court in 1946, however, revealed an incident that cast the former motor transport sergeant in a different light. According to Brett-schneider, on 7 December 1944 Dr Bast had given orders for two imprisoned Slovak insurgents called Ľudovít Hruboň and Pavol Matula to be moved from Rožumberok to another town – Bratislava, Brettschneider thought – with an escort that included SS Hauptscharführer (Master Sergeant) Josef Maurer. Brett-schneider got a lift with them. The truck stopped in a piece of woodland in the municipality of Hrboltová, not far from Rožumberok, and the Germans, five in all, one carrying a spade, went into the wood with the two Slovaks. They came back about forty minutes later without the prisoners. The interpreter noticed that Maurer was now wearing the expensive shoes Hruboň had had on before. The bodies were later found by forestry workers and buried in Hrboltová's graveyard.

After the war, only a few of Sonderkommando 7a's men openly confessed to taking part in the shootings of Jews. 'I thought the orders to liquidate the Jews were right,' former SS Untersturm-führer Willi Dadischek testified in 1961. 'And I did not suffer any doubts when I had to take part in the executions myself. I was entirely of the view that everything the state leadership decreed concerning the Jews, in particular their extermination, was right. I was of the opinion that the liquidation of the Jews would bene-fit the people and the war aims of the time.'

The former SS Oberscharführer (Senior Sergeant) Ernst Wannert, a storeman in civilian life who was Sonderkommando 7a's 'Expert on Bandit Affairs', could remember specific shootings years later, but only those involving partisans. The storeman said that, in the face of constant guerrilla attacks, members of the Sonderkommando had been selected to catch the partisans. Prisoners would be 'taken without exception to Dr Bast, who decided what was to happen to them'. 'Without exception' they would be imprisoned and interrogated. 'If it emerged that the individual prisoner had taken part in atrocities, Dr Bast, by his power of authority, would give orders for that prisoner to be shot.' As a rule, however, Dr Bast had acted humanely; in particular, he was not a Jew-hater. Once, while they combed through a patch of woodland, eight Jews – men, women and children – had been found and brought to him as senior officer. In the witness's presence Dr Bast had said – word for word – 'Let the poor swine make a run for it!' which they then did.

As I read this, I wondered if that could really have happened; I would have been only too happy to believe it. But how could the storeman remember after so long the exact words with which my father supposedly gave the Jews their freedom? It is possible that he wasn't lying, and equally possible that he wanted, understandably from his point of view, to cast a milder light on events in Slovakia during the war. He was after all giving a statement to the police in 1971. His credibility as a witness is further compromised by the fact that he said that 'he never knew of' any killings of Jews or other civilians in Slovakia.

The German troops, supported by the Einsatzgruppen and units of the Waffen SS, brought the Slovak uprising under control by the end of October 1944 but, rather than capitulate, the insurgents retreated to the mountains and shifted to guerrilla warfare. On 16 January 1945 members of Sonderkommando 7a, supported by Billerbeck Company, searched the area around Donovaly, south of Ružomberok, for partisans and Jews in hiding. The mountain villages lay under deep snow. In Weiler Bully they found seven Jews hidden in Karolína Bullová's house, a single-storey rough stone hut. They burnt them alive in the house with Karolína Bullová. More Jews were discovered in the house of Františka Bullová, who the villagers called 'Regina'. They were shot and the house burnt to the ground as well. The Germans did the same in Weiler Polianka: they found a number of Jews in František Bulla's house who they shot along with František's wife, Lína Bullová. In all twenty-one people were murdered that day.

When I arrived in Donovaly, I looked for the graves of Karolína and Lína Bullová in the cemetery next to the road. I walked between the rows of wrought-iron crosses and gravestones, many of which bore the names Bulla or Bullová and pious inscriptions such as '*Nech je im zem slovenksá l'ahka!*' ('May the Slovak earth lie light upon you!'), but I couldn't find the two brave women's graves. A stooped old man was carrying water to a fresh grave in a yellow plastic watering can; out of the corner of my eye I saw that the name Bullová was painted on the wooden cross. A few rusted crosses stood in tall grass in the old part of the cemetery; time and rain had washed the names from their plaques.

I sat down on a bench near the cemetery and took out the protocol, which I had discovered in the archive in Banská Bystrica. It had been drawn up in Donovaly on 18 January 1945 in the presence of a local councillor, Anton Longauer, the local priest, Reverend Father Vojtěch Kambala, the headmaster of the elementary school, Rudolf Čunderlík, and an inhabitant of Donovaly called Ludvik Miartuš to establish the identities of the people who had been murdered two days before. The inexperienced autopsists recorded every piece of information they could about the horrifically damaged human remains that lay before them in the fresh January snow.

'Kollárová, between 140–150 centimetres tall, dark skin, red blouse, around 35 years old. Israelite religion.' She had no personal papers on her. Her son and husband were also among the dead; the protocol recorded that her son was shot in his pyjamas. The identification of her husband was only provisional, the body was so charred. Júlia Sairingerová, Jewish, from Bratislava, died wearing a coffee-coloured dress and a jacket the same colour. She was shot in František Bulla's house. The villagers could not identify some of the dead: two men, one around 170 centimetres, the other, whose body still bore the remains of a black pinstripe suit, slightly taller; a girl, around 150 centimetres, and a woman with a black cotton coat and boots. These were the only distinguishing characteristics of these victims.

Mrs Mlynárová, the mother of a well-known doctor from Prešov, was wearing long green stockings when she died. She was shot in František Bulla's house too, along with a nameless man approximately thirty-five years old with chestnut brown hair and a grey-haired woman whose age the witnesses estimated at fifty. According to the locals a grandmother and a married couple with two sons had lived in the Bullas' house. All the murdered were of the Jewish faith, with the exception of the two Bullovás, who, since their identities had been established beyond doubt, were not laid out in the snow in front of the horrified villagers. Only thirteen of the nineteen Jewish victims could be identified. The dead were then taken to a field belonging to a Polianka farmer that the locals called *Horárska lúka*, Forester Meadow, and there laid to rest in a common grave.

I went back to my car. It was Sunday and Donovaly was deserted. Two buzzards flew in wide circles over a nearby mountain ridge, uttering plaintive cries. Here and there among the dull, wintry green of the woods larches shone like blazing yellow torches.

At the end of January and the start of February 1945 Sonderkommando 7a was transferred by stages to Žilina, north-west of Rožumberok. Before leaving, it liquidated all the prisoners in the Old Fort. Russia, Poland, Slovakia – it was always the same. The Sonderkommando left behind scorched earth and mass graves, murdering its prisoners before pulling out. On 20 January twenty-two prisoners – partisans, with two young women among them – were taken from Rožumberok to the village of Lisková four kilometres away and shot on a wooded hill called Medzihrádky. On 26 January eight prisoners were shot in a wood near the village of Likavka. The bodies were found by locals and buried in the village cemetery. On 2 February, when most of the Sonderkommando was already in Žilina, a further fourteen prisoners were taken to the municipality of Lucky, north-east of Rožumberok, and shot in the back of the neck in the woods near Šiare. Other prisoners were shot in Rožumberok itself.

In May 1945, after the Red Army had liberated the town on the Váh, a terrible discovery was made in the courtyard of the Old Fort. The hurriedly retreating Germans had left behind mounds of rubbish. An officer gave orders for a pit to be dug to dispose of it. Soon after starting to dig, the Russians discovered bits of clothing, shoes, cutlery, rucksacks and other utensils, and underneath these two layers of clothed bodies that had been laid on top of each other, the heads of those on top by the feet of those below to save space. The Einsatzgruppen called this the 'sardine method'. All the bodies lay face down. Twenty-two were found in all, fourteen women and eight men. A doctor reported that they had all been shot in the back of the head and, judging by the degree of decomposition, that they must have been in the pit for several months. They were presumably shot in December 1944 or January 1945 in the cellars of the fort where the prisoners were kept, and blood and bullet holes were found on the walls. The dead were aged between approximately seventeen and fifty. The men were all clearly of Jewish origin and it was thought likely, judging by their appearance, that the women were too. Their clothes were of good quality, suggesting that they had belonged to the middle class; no identity papers were found, only personal items like toothbrushes, a thermos flask, shaving equipment, tobacco and so on. A commission recorded standard distinguishing features, such as physique, hair colour and scars, for possible future identification and took small samples of each person's clothing, which they put in paper bags and numbered. The bags and descriptions of the dead were deposited in the local police station. Each body was denoted by the number of the relevant bag, so that if their identity were ever established, they could be exhumed by relatives. The victims were then buried in two mass graves in the Jewish cemetery in Rybárpole, a suburb of Ružomberok, in the presence of the Russian town commandant, Major Schmelkov, and the Polish-born Rabbi Izrael Leichter. A guard of honour fired three salvoes over the graves, and then the rabbi read a psalm.

None of the twenty-two victims could be identified, suggesting that all their close relatives and friends had died with them.

Sonderkommando 7a spent roughly four weeks in Žilina. During this time the news reached my father that he had been awarded the War Service Cross First Class with swords. At the beginning of March his unit was transferred to Senica, the town where seven months before it had begun its active service in Slovakia. The Red Army was advancing inexorably, to the north through the Dukla Pass and to the east over the Carpathians; the partisans were also stepping up their activities. The German troops and their Slovak allies began preparing to flee. Sonderkommando 7a pulled out of Senica at some point in March 1945 and headed to Brünn, where it was disbanded. Some of the men were sent to Prague, others to Salzburg to reinforce the fabled 'Alpine Redoubt', which in reality existed only in the imaginations of Hitler and his few remaining diehards. My father went to Linz. I haven't been able to establish from documents whether he was acting on orders or whether he issued the order himself.

Shootings, exhumations, detailed records of bodies in mass graves or left unburied in the Old Fort in Ružomberok, on Medzihrádky hill, in Šiare, in Forester Meadow in Donovaly; the itemizing and categorizing of mortal wounds, the description of items of clothing found on the dead, the statements of witnesses, who in many cases had carried out the killings themselves – all the original documents, reports, trial transcripts and file records that I had amassed and read over and over created only blurred images in my mind, like prints prematurely removed from the developing solution which reveal vague outlines but leave the real shape of the figures to the imagination. Wandering between the overgrown graves in Donovaly graveyard, pushing aside clumps of grass, it had occurred to me that my work was like trying to read the names on the crosses – I was trying to decipher something that would always remain fragmentary. At that moment I understood that I would never be able to find an answer to the question that tormented me: how it could have happened that it was my father, of all people, who had ordered these things 'by his power of authority' and perhaps pulled the trigger himself. My father, the Sturmbannführer, who decades afterwards that ex-sergeant said had always acted humanely. What did 'humanely' mean in the language of these people?

What would have happened if . . .? This most meaningless of all questions has left me no peace either, since I tentatively began working on this book years ago, then broke off, then finally took it up again. What would have happened if my great-grandfather Paul Bast, who moved from the Rhineland to Tüffer in the middle of the nineteenth century, had married a Slovene instead of a German? If the family had become Slovenian, as many in the area did? Did everything really begin in the little market town of Tüffer in Lower Styria, where rabid nationalism poisoned the co-existence of Germans and Slovenes? Or did something happen later that sent the whole family down that path of hatred and violence, which reached its unfathomable culmination in my father's Nazi career?

I discovered a photograph of some of the people who the villagers of Lisková had found dead on the Medzihrádky hill and buried in the village graveyard in January 1945. It was in an exhibition in the Museum of the Slovak National Uprising in Banská Bystrica, at which I was the only visitor. A member of the museum staff had opened the exhibition especially for me. An attendant followed me at a slight distance, turning on the lights in each room as I came to it. The exhibition contained enlarged copies of documents and photographs, uniforms, pieces of equipment belonging to the insurgents and the Germans and, in particular, large numbers of weapons, from homemade pistols and hand grenades to machine guns and light artillery. In display case No. 37 I saw a photograph, numbered No. 18, among uniforms, old pistols and other military objects. According to the key at the corner of the display case, it was a picture of people who had been shot by members of Sonderkommando 7a in January 1945 on Medzihrádky hill.

The photograph shows the heads and upper bodies of several corpses; one can't tell how many exactly since they are lying in part on top of one another. Coincidentally or deliberately, the heads are arranged in what is very nearly a star shape. At the cen-

tre of this grotesque tableau is the face of a beautiful young woman with dark hair who could be sleeping peacefully, her expression is so relaxed, were another dead person – it is impossible to tell whether it is a man or a woman – not lying across her breast, his or her mouth opened wide in a scream. A few inches away from the dark-haired woman lies another body of unidentifiable gender, their heads touching, almost like those of two living people lying in the grass and looking at the clouds. The body, whose teeth are bared in a horrifying grin, seems as far as one can tell to be naked, whereas the young woman and the body lying on top of her are wearing clothes.

For the first time, I saw actual victims of my father and of the men under his command, and I discovered their contorted, beautiful faces.

23

My mother's marriage was dissolved in March 1945. My stepfather
filed for a divorce at Linz regional court on the grounds of adultery, but this was simply a formality to resolve the situation
quickly. My mother wanted to marry another man, my father,
and my stepfather didn't want to stand in their way. The divorce
must have been consensual, otherwise how can one explain the
fact that my stepfather was represented by the Amstetten attorney
Dr Rudolf Bast, my grandfather and the father of the man with
whom my mother had committed adultery? Perhaps the arrangement was designed to minimize costs, apart from keeping everything in the family.

On 17 April 1945 my parents were married at Linz registry office.
It was not a good time to be embarking on a new life. The
Gauleiter of Upper Danube, August Eigruber, issued an overblown
appeal on the radio on the same day, declaring that 'the hour of the
decisive battle' had come. In fact, the outcome of the battle had
been decided long before and not even the 'mobile courts martial'
created by Eisgruber to round up 'deserters and malingerers' and
shoot them on the spot could do anything to change that.

The 'Third Reich' my father had served with blind loyalty was
on the verge of collapse. To the east, Soviet troops had crossed the
Austrian border on 29 March 1945, captured Vienna by mid-April
and, continuing to advance westwards, reached the area around
Amstetten. To the west American troops were in Bavaria and, to
the north, in Thüringen. Upper Austria, where food was more
plentiful than in most other areas behind the front, was overrun
with columns of refugees – ethnic Germans from Transylvania

and Hungary, people who had been bombed out of Vienna and other cities, fugitives from the advancing Soviet army. By April the Slovak President Jozef Tiso and his entire government, having fled Bratislava, were billeted in the Kremsmünster monastery in the foothills of the Alps. Only the Slovak Minister of the Interior and the Supreme Commander of the Hlinka Guard, Šano Mach (whom my father had had dinner with four months before in the Arts Centre in Rožumberok), had separate quarters in Traunkirchen in the Salzkammergut. The Russians occupied Bratislava on 4 April.

Upper Austria had become a target for Allied air raids, which concentrated on the industrial areas of Linz, Steyr and Wels, long before it saw any foreign troops. On 16 December 1944 our house in Linz was destroyed by American bombers. Our maid Resi and I were in the cellar when the house collapsed, and we were apparently trapped there for a day and a half.

The destruction of the house was often talked about later: the countless pictures and prints of my stepfather that were lost, the valuable Persian carpets and other furnishings that were burnt. But no one spoke of the air raid itself, the bombs falling, the search for people trapped in the rubble, as if they weren't worth mentioning. I don't know whether everybody was in the cellar when the bombs fell, or – if it was just Resi and I – where the others (my stepfather, my mother, my half-brother and half-sister) were and who pulled us out of the rubble. The destruction caused by the air raids became a taboo subject in post-war Germany and Austria, about which, by tacit and universal agreement, as W. G. Sebald put it in *On the Natural History of Destruction*, nothing could be said or written. What was talked and written about endlessly was the heroic task of reconstruction.

I found an article in a Linz local paper from 1950 about the artist Hans Pollack, my stepfather, which praised the indomitable willpower that saw him 'take a pickaxe and shovel into his hands' as early as May 1945 and, 'an ascetic figure in those hungry years', embark on clearing away the traces of destruction and begin rebuilding. 'The first stage was to clean and dress 36,000 bricks, every single one of which went through his hands. The sheer heroism of this work was rewarded in 1949 when he was able to bring his wife and children home to Linz and begin a "new life" in a new studio.'

I only found out that Resi and I were trapped for hours in the bombed house while I was working on this book, in a file on my Amstetten grandfather, who mentioned it in passing in a statement to court. Nor was the divorce shortly after the house had been destroyed alluded to, either at the time or in later versions of family lore; it was an episode that couldn't be squared with the narrative of the intact family being brought home to Linz after the house had been rebuilt. I still don't know how long after my natural father died my mother remarried my stepfather.

The report in the Linz paper was illustrated with a drawing of the destroyed house by my stepfather. A ruin, it is still just about possible to recognize that it was once two-storeyed; the left side has completely caved in and a surviving chimney sticks up through bare rafters. Of the right-hand façade, only a wall remains, like a panel of a stage set. For some reason he has dated the picture: 25 April 1945, exactly a week after the woman he loved and was deeply devoted to married someone else. It is remarkable that in that situation he had the strength and presence of mind to record the annihilation of his own home. After the bombing, my mother first went to my grandparents in Amstetten with my two siblings and me. But Amstetten wasn't safe ground either; it was as much a target for Allied bombers as Linz, and the Red Army was not far away. My mother then fled back to Upper Austria to Hofkirchen, a tiny place in the Mühlviertel, with my grandparents, who, as well-known Nazis, had good reason to fear the Russians. Before they left Amstetten, my grandparents destroyed any incriminating evidence: swastika flags, pictures of Hitler and documents, presumably including papers of my father. Grandfather wrapped his guns in oilcloths and buried them in a place he would later search for in vain. We only stayed in Hofkirchen for a short time; the Mühlviertel (the part of Upper Austria north of the Danube) became a Russian occupation zone, like all of Lower Austria.

My grandparents went from there to Oftering, a hamlet just south of Linz, where they found lodgings with farmers. My mother was evacuated with her children to a remote little place in Ennstal in Styria where we spent the next couple of years.

My parents married at a time of total collapse and random flight through a country dissolving into chaos: my mother with three small children, aged five, three and one, going from Linz to Amstetten, from Amstetten to Hofkirchen, from Hofkirchen to Linz, from Linz to Mitterberg, my father knowing that at any moment he could be arrested as a war criminal. It is hard to comprehend what can have induced him to marry in circumstances like this and claim responsibility for a woman with three children. He had given 13 Langgasse, Linz, as his address at the wedding, the headquarters of the Gestapo whose chief he had been until he was sent east. I can't say whether he worked for them again after his return from Slovakia; I only know that 13 Langgasse was completely destroyed a week after the wedding by a direct hit during an air raid. Over fifty members of the Secret State Police, including the then chief, a certain Dr Leopold Spann, were killed.

I have never seen any photos of my parents' wedding; there probably are none. I imagine it was a hasty affair: there wasn't much to celebrate, nor were the SS in evidence on such occasions any more. To replace the despised church wedding, the Reichsführer of the SS Heinrich Himmler had devised a special 'marriage consecration' for members of his black order, a solemn ritual in which the bride and groom were given bread and salt. But in April 1945 no one had time for such a performance and I doubt if my father even applied for the obligatory marriage permit from the Reich Security Main Office. It can't have been clear how to make such an application in any case. Berlin was falling: the RSHA was within range of Soviet artillery, the bureaucrats of the terror were busy preparing to escape, if they had not already, and SS central administration had collapsed. Heinrich Himmler was trying to open separate negotiations with the western allies through a Swedish diplomat; the chief of the RSHA, the Linz-born Ernst Kaltenbrunner, was hatching fantastic peace plans to save his skin, and Hitler was sitting in his Führer bunker, one moment ranting about a massive counterattack that would utterly wipe out the Russians at the gates of Berlin, and the next talking about suicide, which he eventually committed on 30 April 1945.

I don't know what my father did in the final weeks of the Third Reich or whether he was attached to the Gestapo or the SD. Both organizations moved their archives to Kremsmünster monastery shortly before the end of the war to pulp them and erase the traces of their crimes. Possibly he was sent to the Ausseerland region of Styria, to one of the numerous command posts there in the final phase of the war where prominent members of the regime flocked, as if they actually believed in the mythical Alpine redoubt concocted by Nazi propaganda to frighten the western allies and extract better conditions for peace, both hopes that remained unrealized.

I cannot imagine my father believing in the Alpine redoubt. He knew the area at first hand and must have been aware that no arrangements whatsoever had been made for building a defensive position encompassing the entire Alpine foothills from Amstetten to Linz and Salzburg. There weren't even any concrete plans for the more modest version, the so-called Inner Fortress, let alone any attempts to start the building, which would have taken months, if not years. Hitler gave the definitive order to begin work on the Inner Fortress on 28 April 1945, three days before his suicide. The armistice came into force on 9 May.

My father experienced the regime's last chaotic days and disintegration at close quarters, in the flesh, so it seems all the more surprising that he made hardly any preparations for what would happen afterwards and did not even secure any false papers for his escape, which couldn't have been difficult for a senior Gestapo officer. Did the collapse paralyze his ability to make decisions, was he panic-stricken? Or did he want to hold out to the bitter end? In any case, it didn't occur to him to give himself up and answer for his actions. Other leading Nazis behaved in the same way. The head of the RSHA, Ernst Kaltenbrunner, slunk away with a few close friends and hid in a hunting hut near the Altaussee, where he was run to ground by the Americans a few days later. He had false papers identifying him as an army doctor, but that was the extent of his escape preparations. He gave himself up without a fight.

When my father went into hiding after the end of the war, it was his mother who begged relatives and friends to get papers for her son. A young female relative went to a registration office for ethnic German refugees in Linz and pretended to be a Sudeten German. She told me that there was a civil servant in a tiny room engrossed in writing something, with a pile of blank identity-card forms on the desk in front of him. She made up some story about fleeing from the Sudetenland and, bending towards him as she spoke, put a hand on the pile, palmed one of the forms and then straightened up again. This was the identity card that was found on my father's body in April 1947, made out, presumably by him, in the name of Franz Geyer, a worker from Krško, German name Gurkfeld, in Slovenia.

Of course, it is impossible to tell exactly why he chose the name Franz Geyer now, but while I was in Slovenia I came across a baker of *Lebkuchen* (gingerbread) of this name who had founded a brewery in 1825 in a former hospital in Tüffer, which later was taken over by a Slovene, Josef Kuketz. The brewery is still going strong and dominates the town: Laško Pivo (Tüffer Beer) is a huge firm that sells its products all over Slovenia. Tüffer's German residents, traditionally terrific beer drinkers, would certainly have known the name of their local brewing pioneer.

On 2 May 1945, three days before Linz was handed over to the American troops without a fight and a week before the armistice came into force, my father was in Bad Ischl. He recorded the place and date in the will he wrote there. One handwritten sheet of a few lines appointing me sole heir to all his belongings and assets, not that that meant anything, since by the time of his violent death on the Brenner he did not own much more than the clothes he stood up in. His parents' house in Amstetten, where most of his things were stored, was looted after my grandparents fled. In his will he also expressed the wish that I should eventually adopt his surname, which, after considering it for a time, I decided not to do.

I lose track of him in Bad Ischl. He must have wandered through occupied Austria for almost a year after that, permanently looking for places to hide, for somewhere where no one knew him and his past wouldn't be his undoing. In the journal in which he recorded his experiences in the mountains I found a few short notes on the last page that must come from the time when he was on the run. The names of a few Slovenes from Laško who he probably expected to help him (Slovenes of all people, who had been so tormented by the National Socialists), as well as a route, using only side roads, from St Veit on the River Glan in Carinthia to Ennstal, the place to which we had been evacuated.

My mother was sent with her three children to stay on a remote farm in a little municipality called Mitterberg am Grimming. The farmer's family was big – five children – and friendly, and there was another refugee family, ethnic Germans, living there too. My stepfather often visited from Linz and stayed with us for weeks at a time. Only just divorced, he and my mother resumed living together, at least to all outward appearances. I don't think that anyone apart from the two of them knew that they were even divorced. Perhaps they remarried immediately after my father's death, when they were still in Styria. I have asked my brother, but he doesn't know either.

At some point my father appeared in the area. He tried to find work as a woodcutter, but everyone knew what the scars on his face meant: a member of a student duelling fraternity, a pan-German nationalist, a Nazi looking for a hiding place – a war criminal, in other words. He knew the area around Mitterberg from earlier mountaineering trips – the Planner hut, which he had stayed in on frequent skiing holidays, was only a few hours away; perhaps he used it as a place to hide. The would-be forestry worker with the duelling scars immediately aroused suspicion, but before the authorities could take action he had already moved on. I can't say whether he actually visited us; one would think so, but I have no memory of it, just as I don't remember anything about him. I can picture some things from that time quite distinctly, but when I try to conjure up any image of him, nothing comes into my mind.

My memories of our stay on the lonely farm in Mitterberg are faint and sketchy, but they do exist. I remember the cattle shed, the smell and heat of the cows, the farm's dog and, above all, a vicious cock that once, perhaps because I had been teasing one of its hens, flew at my head and pecked me mercilessly until it was shooed off its shrieking victim by a grown-up. One day, when my grandfather came to visit, I climbed a tree, probably to show him how brave and good at it I was, and then didn't dare come back down. The beloved old man, who was over sixty by then, stood at the bottom and shouted at me to come down at once. In the end I lost my grip and fell like a stone, but didn't hurt myself. For some reason the name of an ethnic German boy who lived on the farm with us has stuck in my mind: Uwe Mund. My brother almost shot Uwe's eye out once with a homemade pistol that worked like a catapult and fired wooden darts.

At the start of May 1948, after my father had been dead for over a year, my mother was arrested. She spent two weeks in Graz regional court prison awaiting trial and was then released. I remember two Austrian detectives coming and taking her away in an open-top American jeep – or perhaps someone told me that. The children were supposed to have cried, but I don't remember it. My mother got on well with one of the detectives straightaway. Later he came to visit us in Mitterberg and was a friend of the family until he died.

I have not been able to find out why my mother was arrested, but I presume she helped someone my father knew, a war criminal on the run, or perhaps her name was just found on the fugitive. The man was a senior SS officer from Carinthia called Viktor Nageler, who my father had got to know in Slovakia. Nageler had been an adviser to the Hlinka Guard. After the end of the war he began to recruit former members of the SS in Linz for a neo-Nazi group. He wasn't entirely clear about his plans; perhaps he wanted to set up a wing of the so-called Werewolf Movement. The codename he chose for himself, Trenck, and for his handful of faithful followers, his 'Pandours', reflected his confusion.[*] In May 1947 Nageler was arrested and put in a labour camp in Salza am Grimming, not far from Mitterberg. He managed to escape, at which point he presumably tried to make contact with my

[*] A local force organized by Baron Trenck on his estates in Croatia in 1741 to combat bands of robbers, the Pandours were enrolled as a regiment in the Austrian army, where they became universally dreaded for their rapacity and brutality. Their name was a synonym for 'brutal Croatian soldier'.

199

mother. He was arrested again at the end of April 1948, and a few days later the police took my mother away. The connection seems clear. I found the details about Trenck and his Pandours in newspaper cuttings among my mother's papers.

Nageler was another longstanding friend of the family. He managed to escape again, after being arrested a second time, and go into hiding in Germany, where he adopted a false name and led a secure bourgeois existence. He was taken on as a sales representative by a renowned German educational publisher. Presumably there was somebody in the upper echelons of the company who at least suspected this Austrian's background. From time to time, now calling himself something different, Nageler visited us in Linz; a tall, self-confident man, every inch the self-proclaimed member of the master race and infinitely vain. Living in north Germany had instilled in him a love for everything he considered truly German: straightforwardness, honesty, firmness. He called the Austrians nerveless, dishonest, lazy, a race of rogues. This native Carinthian said that now he felt completely north German. I remember him once studying himself lovingly in the big mirror in our hall. He ran his fingers through his hair, turned his head to the left, then to the right, straightened his tie, bared his teeth at his reflection and said admiringly, 'The Admiral.' He would have liked that rank. I think he had been a secondary-school teacher before rising up the Nazi hierarchy; the success had gone to his head, as with many of his sort.

I haven't been able to find out much about my father's experiences in the months he moved around Allied-liberated Austria as a 'U-boat', as people on the run were called. Most of the state's structures had collapsed, which would have made it easier to disappear, and there were up to a million so-called Displaced Persons in Austria: prisoners released from concentration camps, former forced labourers, ethnic Germans driven out of, or fleeing from, eastern Europe, citizens of Hitler's former allies who didn't want to return to their countries. Many had suspect papers or none at all, but none had the duelling scars on their face, that tell-tale mark of the nationalist fraternity member, of whom most had been radical National Socialists. Between 1938 and 1945 a scarred face had been a badge of the élite; now for many it had become a curse. One could take off the uniform and, if need be, get rid of the SS tattoo, contemptuously called the 'SS brand' by soldiers (although that sort of scarring was suspicious), but duelling scars couldn't be surgically removed. They were inherently incriminating, especially when the bearer sought to pass himself off as a simple worker or woodcutter.

My father couldn't expect any help from his parents, either, who were still living in Oftering just south of Linz. The Austrian and American authorities had my grandfather in their sights as an ardent National Socialist, from when the party was still outlawed, a Nazi functionary (Leader of the NSDAP District Legal Office in Amstetten) and a suspected war criminal. He was recognized in Linz station on 21 September 1945 and handed over to the CIC, US Army Counterintelligence, who put him in the Marcus W. Orr internment camp in Glasenbach near Salzburg. Over 10,000 National Socialists were held there, mainly Austrians but also former German generals (most notably Albert Kesselring, the former army commander in Italy), Croats, Hungarians, Serbs and Slovaks, including the puppet Prime Minister Jozef Tiso.

The Americans had put my grandfather on their list for allegedly participating in a violent attack on captured American pilots in Amstetten in March 1945. Amstetten had been subjected to a heavy air raid on 20 March, as a result of which a train was forced to wait in the station for a considerable amount of time. Among the passengers were fifteen American prisoners of war on their way to Frankfurt. When they were marched across the main square, a crowd of enraged party officials, women and men alike, gathered and began to beat the Americans with fists, shovels and sticks; one man even had a whip. The escort's attempts to protect their prisoners had no effect on the mob. It seems almost miraculous, given the weapons the mob were using, that none of the Americans died. Witnesses claimed to have seen my grandfather among the frenzied attackers.

He was brought to trial in Salzburg before an American Special Military High Tribunal in January 1947, along with twenty-four other Amstetten residents. He denied taking any part in the lynching, claiming that because it was his wife's birthday that day he had had a large lunch at home and only later gone to the main square when their maid told him what was happening. It was all over by the time he got there, so he went to a pub for a round of schnapps, where he expressed his outrage at the maltreatment of the prisoners of war. This version could not be disproved and my grandfather was acquitted. There were ten acquittals in all, and fifteen Amstetten residents were sentenced to forced labour. The entire proceedings were conducted so correctly and fairly, according to an Amstetten newspaper, 'that it must have amazed onlookers when they thought that the Americans were judging people who had assaulted their compatriots'.

My grandfather's fair treatment and acquittal were not enough, however, to alter the sweeping judgement that, even years later, was passed on Americans in the Bast household: the Americans were swine! As far as I know, it was never explained why they were all swine; it was simply an article of unassailable doctrine, comparable to the statement that our earth is a sphere, not a plane. The earth is a sphere, and the Americans are swine.

My grandfather was acquitted in Salzburg of maltreating the prisoners of war but not released. Instead he was handed over to the American Military Tribunal in Nuremberg, which held him for a while and then sent him back to the Glasenbach internment camp. I presume he was too minor for Nuremberg. He was eventually handed over to the Vienna Regional Superior Court, where he was tried before the People's Court Tribunal on a charge of high treason regarding his membership of the NSDAP in the 1930s, when it was a banned organization in Austria. Membership of the outlawed party automatically qualified as high treason.

Under questioning my grandfather claimed that he had not joined the NSDAP until after the Anschluss; 1931 was simply the year his membership had been backdated to after he made his lavish contribution to party funds. No one believed this explanation; it was exposed in countless ways, not least by the NSDAP personnel questionnaire that he had personally filled out shortly after the Anschluss, which was submitted to the court. There he had proudly listed all the services he had rendered the outlawed party: he had collected dues for the local party branch and the Amstetten SS office, represented fellow party members in court free of charge, drafted complaints, appeals and objections, and actually taken the trouble to engage in extensive correspondence with other lawyers on these matters, including Arthur Seyss-Inquart, the overall head of the Austrian Nazis. Naturally he had also helped comrades in prison with money and gifts in kind and regularly contributed to the banned Nazi charity, the NS-Winterhilfe.

A founder member of the Austrian Nazis, in short, who had tirelessly and selflessly devoted himself to the party. After 1945 everything was very different.

Although my grandfather had obviously lied at his trial, he was released from prison after a week and allowed to return to Oftering. He had been in custody for around two years in all, in Linz, Glasenbach, Nuremberg and Vienna Regional Superior Court. I was told later that he changed a great deal over that period. I found submissions written by him in a shaky scrawl in his file from the People's Court Tribunal. He suffered from dilation of the heart and extensive cardiac muscle damage, hypertrophy of the liver (presumably a consequence of his drinking) and emphysema, coupled with severe depression after his son's murder, which he had found out about while he was in prison in Nuremberg. In addition, he had had an accident driving a little horse-drawn carriage, a gig, in Oftering, which left him with a couple of broken ribs. He had sought to explain his politics in an incorrigible statement to court.

> I was born in Tüffer, which is now in Yugoslavia, and so I am a language-border German, having spent my youth in those parts until my 30th year. Throughout that time, a bitter struggle raged between us Germans and the Slovenes over our language and our national identity. The natural consequence of this struggle was that we ethnic Germans always became nationalists – long before there was any sign of the NSDAP – and remained so. We never had any truck with 'turncoats' as they are called; such a thing was completely and utterly alien to us.

So everything had begun in Tüffer in Lower Styria at the end of the nineteenth century. He wrote this in 1948. Just before that I went to stay with him for a few months, while my grandmother was in Amstetten trying to get their house back from the Russians; my half-brother and sister were sent somewhere else. He was a sick, embittered old man, an obsessive Nazi, anything but an ideal person to look after a child, but I have only good memories of him. He told me stories about his childhood in Tüffer and the hunting in Gottschee and the bears and wolves. We walked over the fields and he showed me how to whittle a little pipe from willow and how to fish. From Oftering I went to stay in Amstetten with my grandmother, who had finally managed to get a flat in her own house after petitioning for one for a long time. The high treason case against my grandfather dragged on half-heartedly until 1950, when a presidential pardon caused it to be dropped.

Like most Austrian Nazis he got off lightly in the end. There was no moral insight, or plain remorse, on his part. No doubt any expression of regret would have made him a 'turncoat' of the sort he found inconceivable. But nor were he and his like asked to change their beliefs. Around this time the main Austrian political parties, the ÖVP, the Austrian People's Party, and the SPÖ, the Austrian Socialist Party, resumed canvassing former National Socialists, who represented a large potential constituency for them.

In September 1955, the year of the Austrian State Treaty that finally settled the country's status, Amstetten's Russian commandant released the last flat in my grandparents' building, which was itself one of the last things to be requisitioned by the Russians. The release came after long negotiations with the municipal authorities over compensation for alleged losses from looting and other damage sustained during the occupation. The flat was inspected, records were compiled, people who might be able to say what my grandparents had owned before 1945 were questioned. One of them was the vet Hans Schutting, who had gone hunting with my grandfather for years. Herr Schutting was expected to supply information about the furnishings of my grandparents' flat but he was not very helpful. He couldn't say what furniture there'd been in the dining room, living room or smoking room, or even how many people had lived in my grandfather's house. All he knew was that my grandfather and his family were simply and neatly dressed. Of all the household's contents, he could only remember one thing, a sporting gun, as if the whole flat, where he had so often been entertained as a guest, had contained nothing except this gun. But Herr Schutting could describe it down to the last detail. It was a Sauer and Son sixteen-bore shotgun with side locks and a Damascus steel barrel, virtually brand new. In his opinion the occupying power had taken it.

My grandfather always spoke of his hunting friend Hans

Schutting with great respect; they shared a passion for hunting and for guns. I met the vet on a number of occasions in Amstetten and remember him as a blustering man with a deep voice dressed in hunting clothes and high boots who made me feel slightly afraid.

24

The South Tyrolean municipality of Olang, which is called Valdaora in Italian,* is in Hochpustertal, at the foot of the Kronplatz mountain and the foothills of the Pragser Dolomites. The municipality consists of four villages – Oberolang, Mitterolang, Niederolang and Geiselbirg – each with its own church. My father reached the area on the run in 1946 and found work and board as a farmhand in Niederolang. Johann Brunner's farm was the largest in Olang and the surrounding area, with extensive woods, mountain pastures and around twenty head of cattle. I have not been able to find out which route my father took to get to the South Tyrol or how he travelled, whether by foot or bicycle or some other way.

By pure chance I came across an old villager on a visit to Niederolang who could remember the stranger who had worked as a farmhand for Johann Brunner. When I showed him various photos of my father, he recognized him in one where he was climbing a mountain, wearing an old felt hat, perhaps of the sort he wore in Olang. The old man said that it had been obvious right away that the stranger hadn't grown up working on a farm or in the forest. He was always friendly, but he was quiet. He had hardly any contact with people outside the farm; he never went into the village, to the pub or the church, and he never talked about himself. In those days, of course, they worked all day long, from six in the morning until evening prayers at half past six, so they didn't

*Formerly part of the Habsburg Empire, the South Tyrol was annexed to Italy at the end of the First World War, in September 1919, by the treaty of St Germain, and the Brenner Pass then became the border between it and Austria.

have much time to talk. On Saturdays they worked until four; only Sundays were free. The stranger had said he was a German soldier, but the old man said that personally he thought he was an officer judging by his appearance and manner; he was a dashing man. He couldn't remember the stranger's name, but he had a small room on the farm and ate with the other farmhands. Every morning there was brown roux soup and *mus*, a boiled-milk pudding with melted butter that was put on the table in a big pan and everyone helped themselves from that. They only had coffee with milk on Sundays. The old man said that it was winter then and they had spent most of the time felling trees and getting them down off the mountain. Hard, dangerous work. They brought the timber – sometimes logs over four metres long – down on sleds ridden by one person, who had to be very strong and skilful since the loads were heavy and the path steep and twisting. One day the stranger, who anyway took less because he wasn't used to the work, had an accident on his way down. At a place called Pracken Wood he braked too late on a sharp turn and the heavy load slammed him into a fence. He was taken down to the valley and the farmer drove him to hospital in Bruneck, where he stayed for some time. When he came back, he had trouble walking and had to use a stick, so he did lighter work about the farm, wood chopping and so on.

The accident explains why my father spent so long in Niederolang. He had to wait until he recovered from his injuries and could walk properly again. At some point at the start of 1947 – the old man couldn't say when exactly – he left the farm with his possessions, mainly food, in a woven basket on his back, which he had bought from a local weaver. When word came later that the stranger had been shot on the Brenner Pass, the old man said he felt sorry, because he had got on well with him. Some time later, evidently having found out that he'd worked there, the police came to the farm and asked around.

I didn't find any more references to the woven basket the old man told me about; it never came up again. Perhaps my father only took it with him as camouflage, thinking that a man with a basket on his back would be taken for a local, and then got rid of it, exchanged it perhaps, so it wouldn't get in his way crossing the border.

As far as I can tell he must have set out for the Brenner Pass from Niederolang at the beginning of March. He wanted to slip across the border to meet my mother, who was in Innsbruck, waiting for news of him. I don't know what his plans were after that; presumably he intended to go overseas somehow, like so many other Nazis wanted for war crimes. Perhaps he wanted to make contact with accomplices from Innsbruck who could set him up with new papers and money and organize the next stage of his journey. He can't have been carrying much money: it would have been too risky if he was stopped by the police and he may not have had much cash in any case. But a letter from Linz Police Head Office to the Public Prosecutor's Office in May 1946 mentions eleven places in different Austrian municipalities where Dr Gerhard Bast ('an extremely fanatical and brutal person who will shrink at nothing') had allegedly hidden objects of value, although the letter doesn't give any sources for this information.

On 8 or 9 March he reached Brennerbad, close to the border. It was common knowledge that it was watched closely, so he looked for a guide he could pay to get him across. It wasn't hard to find one. Plenty of locals in the tough post-war years earned their living and more by smuggling. Anything that could be bartered or sold at a profit was smuggled: saccharin and silk stockings, drugs and coffee, medicine and livestock, ox hides and fur coats, foreign currency and gold. There was a traffic in people too. The South Tyrol was swarming with individuals who wanted to get over the border, some heading south, to Italy and beyond, others north, to Austria and Germany: Displaced Persons looking for a new home, eastern European Jews fleeing communism and re-awakened anti-Semitism whom Jewish escape organizations would take to Palestine, Nazi war criminals who were passed along the 'Rat Line'* to Rome, provided with new identities and papers by sympathizers in the Vatican, and then shipped on, generally to South America.

My father hired the twenty-five-year-old Rudolf G., a labourer from Brennerbad, as his guide. Later it emerged that locals had warned him against the young man. G. was known as an unreliable, brutal man who it was best to keep clear of. But my father had turned a deaf ear: he was thirty-six, athletic and strong; what harm could a young ruffian do him? They set off late in the evening on 9 March, a Sunday. Accounts differ as to which route

*Escape route run by US Army Counterintelligence, which most famously smuggled Klaus Barbie to Bolivia in 1951.

Rudolf G. took. Some say he chose a narrow hunting path along the steep east slope, whilst a newspaper later reported that they took the road. In any case Rudolf G. walked a few paces in front of my father. They had almost reached the Brenner Pass when G. suddenly drew a pistol, turned and shot him in the chest. G. then dragged his body to a nearby bunker he knew from his smuggling trips. There he realized that the man was still showing signs of life, so he shot him twice in the head at close range. He searched his clothes and rucksack, which contained dirty washing and some food. The spoils were meagre: 3,000 lire, 20 schillings, a watch and a gold ring. He went home after the murder, getting rid of the pistol on the way. Rudolf G. confessed to all this when he was arrested in Brixen in April 1947, four weeks after the murder.

The arrest came a few days after the discovery of the body. Suspicion had immediately fallen on the young man, the *carabinieri* presumably having been tipped off by the locals. After his arrest, the newspapers wrote that these were not the *carabinieri*'s first dealings with the young man: he was suspected of having robbed people trying to cross the border illegally several times before, but everybody had been too scared to report him to the police. When questioned, Rudolf G. confessed immediately. The man who had claimed to be Franz Geyer had said that he had been staying in Pustertal since October 1946 and now wanted to go to Innsbruck to meet his wife, with whom he planned to emigrate to Canada. G. said that he had assumed that the stranger was carrying a lot of cash and so decided to kill him, but he had not found the money he was hoping for.

Rudolf G. was put in Trento prison. When he began to exhibit certain behavioural disorders in custody, he was sent for tests to a mental institution, where he tried to take his life by slashing his wrists. This was reported by a local newspaper when he was finally tried before a jury in Bolzano in March 1949, two years after the murder. He faced a further charge of attempted robbery, also on the Brenner. The accused looked distracted throughout the trial and gave stock answers to every question: he knew nothing, he hadn't done anything, he couldn't remember anything. He said that he couldn't have done anything anyway because he was very ill. A marshal of the *carabinieri* called Leonarduzzi testified that Rudolf G. had confessed to the crime immediately after his arrest and had seemed completely normal at the time.

After a day's trial, Rudolf G. was found guilty of murder, robbery and attempted robbery and sentenced to thirty years' imprisonment and a fine of 18,000 lire. After serving his sentence he was to be sent to reform school for three years.

When I drove to the South Tyrol in the early summer of 2003, one of the things I hoped to do was track down the man who had shot my father and hidden his body in a bunker fifty-six years before. Enquiries led me to the G. family, who ran a large farm at the foot of the western slope of the Pustertal valley, between the villages of Pontigl and Brennerbad. A sign with the farm's name indicated a turn off onto a private road; another warned of a fierce dog, which was lying asleep under a spreading tree on a long chain as I drove in. Awakened by my footsteps, it jumped up and barked dutifully a few times, before amicably starting to wag its tail. An elderly woman with a tanned face was raking up freshly mown grass and putting it in a wheelbarrow. She was wearing a headscarf and blue overalls and smiled at me. When I asked her if she knew a man called Rudolf G., she raised a hand warily and then nodded: 'Yes, but he's not alive any more.' When did he die, I asked. 'Seven or eight years ago, it may even be ten already.' She wanted to know why I was interested in Rudolf G. I started to explain that it was a long time ago, a crime that had been committed just after the war. She said she had heard about it but she couldn't tell me much: it was long before her time. She asked what I had to do with it. I explained that I was the son of the man who had been killed. 'Jessass Maria,' she gasped and looked at me horrified.

A light breeze blew down from the Brenner. The freshly mown grass smelled strong and aromatic. The dog had fallen asleep again. 'That was a long time ago,' the woman said eventually. 'People used to talk about it a lot at one time but now it's been forgotten.' I asked what people used to say about it. 'That the two of them had got into a fight, apparently because one of them – your father,' she added quickly, '– didn't want to pay the agreed price.' But that was all she could say. Rudolf G. was her brother-in-law; she had married his younger brother, who had been just a child then; she had never seen her brother-in-law. He did not come back home after his prison sentence. When he was released, he moved to Meran, where he married and found a good job and is now buried.

A few days later her husband gave me a slightly different version of the events of March 1947. We stood on the same spot where I had talked with his wife; this time she wasn't to be seen. The dog was excited, running around off the chain and jumping up at me repeatedly before the man shooed it away. He was heavily built and wore worker's overalls and held a drill in his hands all the time we talked.

He said that at that time there were lots of people in the area who wanted to get over the border, soldiers and all different sorts, some wanting to get in, some to get out. Back then his family lived above Brennerbad and there'd often be ten or twelve people sitting in their front room waiting to be taken across; he'd done it himself, although he was not much more than a child at the time. He couldn't remember my father, there had been so many of them, but his brother had set off with him on the usual smugglers' path. A quarrel had broken out near the border because the stranger had refused to pay the agreed sum. One thing had led to another and then the stranger had drawn a pistol, but his brother had been quicker with his gun and shot him. 'Otherwise he would have been dead,' he added after a pause.

213

'Those were bad times,' he said. So in his opinion it was self-defence, I asked. 'Yes, self-defence,' he said. 'My brother was always a good, decent man.' I asked him why, then, didn't his brother say anything about my father's gun or self-defence to the *carabinieri* or later at his trial in Bolzano? He shrugged his shoulders. 'Everyone had a gun then,' he said. 'A person's life wasn't worth much.' He was breathing heavily; the heat seemed to be taking it out of him. Large beads of sweat stood out on his flushed forehead. He said that his brother was in Russia in the war and then they sent him to the southern Italian front. 'It was fierce there too.' He ran his hand over his face several times and wiped the sweat off on his grey wool trousers, which seemed much too hot for a summer day. Finally he repeated, 'My brother was good and decent.' It sounded defiant. I thought of what my grandmother used to say about my father: 'He was always honourable and decent.'

We stood looking at one another in silence for a few minutes, but there wasn't anything else to say. I returned to my car and drove back to the bunker where my father had been found. From the road I could see the stones flanking the entrance under the spruces, the sign with the bilingual inscription and the gate that looked as if it was made of rock but which I knew was made of glass-fibre matting. I didn't get out, but carried on down to Innsbruck.

ACKNOWLEDGEMENTS

This book would never have come about without many people's support. I can only mention a few names here, but I am very grateful to everyone who gave me valuable information and advice while I was carrying out the research and writing of this book. Peter Kaser from Gossensass, a wonderful artist and expert on the fortifications on the Brenner, helped me look for the bunker in which my father was found dead. (He took the photo of the bunker on the cover.) Anton Holzer aided my enquiries in Olang in Pustertal. The Slovenian historian Professor Peter Vodopivec selflessly put his profound learning and time at my disposal, and I am grateful to his colleague Professor Janez Cvirn, who referred me to a great deal of useful literature. My friend Meta Hočevar in Ljubljana was, as ever, a generous host, with whom I was able to have scores of conversations that provided me with constant new insights. My thanks go also to the staff of the Ludwigsburg branch of the German National Archives and of the Museum of the Slovenian Uprising in Banská Bystrica, whose assistance was as friendly as it was professional. While I was working in the Ludwigsburg archives I was lucky enough to enjoy the hospitality of my friend Colin Hainbach.

I was in constant contact with the modern historian Gerhard Zeillinger from the start of my research to the book's completion – he revealed hidden sources, threw open his voluminous and informative archive, was generous with his comprehensive knowledge of the history of Amstetten and his critical awareness of subtleties spared me many embarrassing errors.

Brigitte Hilzensauer was my first, indispensable reader; her unerring literary judgement and staunch support as a friend when I despaired of finishing were invaluable.

My wife has been at my side throughout. She has accompanied me on the trips, buoyed my spirits and never failed to give me heart. I cannot imagine writing anything without her.

My research was assisted by a travel grant from the Sektion für Kunstangelegenheiten of the Austrian Bundeskanzleramt.